Goodness Killed Me!

A story about Love, Money and Exploitation

Er. Ashish Dutt Sharma

DIAMOND BOOKS

ISBN : 978-81-288-3900-9

Publisher : **Diamond Pocket Books (P) Ltd.**
X-30, Okhla Industrial Area, Phase-II
New Delhi-110020
Phone : 011-40712200
E-mail : sales@dpb.in
Website : www.diamondbook.in

Goodness Killed Me!
By - *Er. Ashish Dutt Sharma*

Dedicated to my mother for
her constant love and support.

Acknowledgements

First of all, I would like to thank my worthy readers who would spend their valuable time in reading my first novel. I hope that you would like and understand the work; reading it with the same passion that I have applied to write it. Indirect objective of this writing is to create awareness among typical middle-class society of India especially over-ambitious and strict parents, to show them the results of such attitude and the effects of materialistic globalization on our social lives.

To Dr (Mrs.) Geetika Thapar for motivating me to excel in my work.

Renowned novelist Chetan Bhagat for inspiring me to write.

My mother and family for their constant encouragement and support in my life to do something worthwhile.

My friends and office colleagues, who were instrumental in motivating me to write and share this story with all of you: I am especially thankful to Gurdip Singh, Harjit Singh, Yogesh Kumar, Manu Bansal and Raman

Garg in extending their support throughout and making me feel special. I learnt a lot of things from their lives too.

My students, who like me for my teaching passion and respect me for being a genuine, honest and committed person,

My publishers, who have given me a platform to showcase this story and to make people think before reading and then re-think after reading.

God, who gives me a hope of better tomorrow and a more fulfilling and perfect life. I wish happiness to all.

—Er. Ashish Dutt Sharma

Prologue

I was in New Delhi railway station and about to catch my train *Kalka Shatabdi* for Chandigarh at platform number one. Just in time, I caught my Chair Car; the C2 coach and got inside this beautiful train.

Interiors were royal blue with comfortable seats, window curtains and the coach was so cool from inside even in this hot weather of June month.

I was just looking for my seat number 49, when I saw an old man struggling to put his luggage on the luggage bar above.

"Can I help you sir?" I said after I kept my small bag on the seat.

"Yes please..." the old gentleman replied in exhausted tone.

I helped him put his luggage at the right place and it made him happy.

"Thanks, God bless you young man!" as he sat down in his 48W window seat.

"My seat number is 49..." I said with excitement, "and that's next to you!"

Old man smiled and I sat on my seat.

I saw a very fair and slim young lady with curly brown hair, who was just looking at me with a smiling face. She had just arrived with a coolie and was asking him to put her luggage with the old man's on to the luggage bar.

"So yours seat number forty nine?" the white girl asked.

I said "yeah" and the girl sat on the aisle seat number fifty after she made payment to coolie. I was very happy to sit beside a foreigner.

Train left at exactly the scheduled time of 5:15 pm and water bottles were served first. She took her water bottle and passed on my bottle and the one for old gentleman in the corner seat.

"Your water bottle sir," I said.

"Hey you are a nice guy. I never found someone so caring in your generation," the old man said.

"Thank you sir; I know I am different," I smiled and asked, "Are you also going to Chandigarh?"

"Yes dear, I had to cancel my flight from IGI airport and come back by train due to an urgent work in the office," the old man replied.

"What do you do sir?" I asked in excitement.

"Oh me…? Well, I am the Vice President of ABC group in India. My name is Vikram Kapoor and my head office is in USA," the old man replied.

"Wow, excellent! I also had an opportunity to work abroad and explore different cultures," I said in a formal way while shaking hands with him, "My name is Ashish Dutt."

"Ok Mr. Ashish, I guess you work in some MNC in Delhi?" the old man asked.

"Yes, I used to work for an IT MNC in Gurgaon and now back into education and research field." I replied.

"Ok." the man smiled.

"Can I ask you something as you are an experienced person?" I said.

"Yes, please go on…"

"Teaching has always been my passion and my need for money had driven me into a different field and now I am back to teaching. I did a lot of switching and not able to find my mental peace or stability. What should I do?" I asked with a sadistic expression.

"Gentleman, what you are doing is to dig a well and go up to some depth. When you see no water coming out, you stop and start digging another well. It makes you learn in the process but the end result is that you are still without water. So, my advice is to dig the well deep enough so that you can fetch water. Go to the maximum extent possible to realize your dreams. Don't leave in between to pursue a fancy looking arena as it may not be that good or suitable for you," Mr. Kapoor replied.

"Yes you are right. But do you mean that I should be more focused on single area and not try anything new?"

"No you must try things. Because if you try, only then there is a fifty-fifty chance that either you will succeed or you fail, but if you don't try at all then all you are sure about is to fail and lose."

"But how do I know beforehand what is good and what is not so good for me to pursue?"

"You have to do research and get that knowledge from someone who has been a practitioner of that particular field. Do your work, follow your *guru* and leave the rest to God."

"Thank you very much sir for that useful and well thought out advice."

"My pleasure indeed, I hope I have answered your doubts."

"Yes sir thanks again."

The girl next to me was writing in her diary about the places she visited in Delhi and her experiences in the journey. She had a travel planner lying beside her.

I was looking at her diary with curiosity only when she said, "I am also going to Chandigarh to meet my grandparents."

"Where are you coming from?"

"I live in Toronto, Canada."

"That's great. So, are you an Indian too?"

"Yes, my origin is India, but I was brought up in Canada only as my parents had moved there a long ago," the girl replied.

"Ok, my name is Ashish and it is indeed a pleasure to meet you!"

She smiled and said, "Same here. My name is Nancy."

Train was moving fast and snacks were served. She was trying to call her grandmother in Chandigarh, but her phone network was creating some trouble.

"You can use my phone if you want to make a call," I said in a happy tone as if I had got a good companion.

"Oh thank you so much," as she took my cell phone and confirmed to her grandmother that she's coming to Chandigarh to meet her that night only.

"Hello, *aaj he aa rahi hu ji…* (I am coming today…)"

"Wow, you can speak Hindi also?" I said in astonishment.

"Yes, a little bit, but I am not so good at Hindi," she replied after finishing her call.

After eating snacks, Mr. Kapoor took a nap as he already looked very tired.

While eating her meal, she asked me to look at some photographs in her diary, "Hey, he's my fiancé and we were celebrating his birthday as you can see in these pictures. How is he?"

I said, "He's very smart and looks cool."

"Yeah, and he is very intelligent too and also loves me so much."

"Great."

And only then we heard heated arguments in our adjacent seat.

An old man was standing and yelling at a youth in the back seat when the young man said, "Sir, please don't move your seat backward as my leg is hurt and it's getting painful to move it much."

Old man replied in very insensitive and rude voice, "then why don't you go in airplane mister? I am dead tired and I need to stretch that bloody seat...and if you don't obey me, I will see you after you get down from train."

Young guy was not scared but the railway inspector came to intervene and transferred his seat to settle the issue.

Nancy said pointing to Mr. Kapoor, "Look at the old guy who was so nice to guide you and that one who got no decency and etiquette."

I said, "Nothing is free. A good person pays a cost for his goodness for others. You are right in your observation. But do you know why people here turn out like this?"

"No, tell me why?"

"See, they are not happy with their lives as they get far less from their life than their life takes away from them. So they remain frustrated which may be due to their poor health in old age or other family and personal problems. Love and Money are two basic necessities of a human being, whose lack makes people turn insane in their ending years when they realize that they could not enjoy their lives and only struggled hard under the systems of this poor and corrupt country."

"Yeah, you are right. India is a sex-starved nation. I was shocked to read a rape case of 2 year old in Delhi in the newspaper today. The culprit should be given harshest possible punishment."

"Do you think that only punishment can solve a crime?"

"No, but at least it can be reduced to certain extent."

"Nancy, tit for tat can never be the solution for such complex problems. Do you think the problem of that frustrated old man or such criminals can be just solved by imposing strict measures or stringent laws? It's easy to judge, but only the wearer knows where the shoe pinches. People lack motivation."

"Oh my God, you are a very interesting person. So, Ashish do you really have any real life experience that you would like to share with me? I know a film producer and I could help you by forwarding your story and then, they can make a movie out of it."

"Yes Nancy, I got a real life account of my very close friend Rahul, who was born in a lower middle class family...," and then I started narrating her full story of the constant ordeal that guy had to face in his life.

One

Rahul, aged 4½ years, used to live with his parents on the ground floor of a big ten *marla* house in Mohali (Punjab) as tenants. Other two-room set on the ground floor was occupied by a family from Uttar Pradesh. Their son Raju and Rahul used to play together.

Rahul was fair, cute and chubby boy while Raju was black and thin.

21st March 1984, 10 AM:

"Stop pulling your sister's hand, she's just a one year old baby. You should love and care for her, but God, you are very naughty. Leave her and don't harass her," Rahul's mother yelled from outside while putting her super clean clothes for drying in the sun, "I will tell your father when he comes back home from work that your son is too mischievous," my mother continued.

Leaving my sister there, I came out of the room and started to play with my neighbor's son, Raju.

"Hey Raju, I got a new toy. Would you play with me?" I asked.

Raju nodded and we took our toy cart upstairs and went on to the roof top.

"My mother keep yelling at me all the times," I said.

"All mothers are like that," Raju replied.

"Ok, let's put some stones in the toy cart and drag its wheels to see how much load it can take."

"I am getting bored and want to play marbles with my friends who are having fun with a puppy down there."

"Okay, go. I don't know how to play marbles."

Raju vanished quickly and I kept playing there when suddenly the main door of that one room set on the top floor opened.

"Oh dear, so lovely boy," a guy in the mid 20s said in a very sweet and soft voice as he came out of his room.

"Can I play with you?" he asked while rolling the wheels of my toy cart.

I kept silent but tried to pull away my toy from him.

"Take some sweets dear" as he started touching me all over, kissed my face and took me in his lap.

My intuition said that the guy won't harm me and I took two toffees from his hand. Then, he took my toy cart inside his room and said, "See my room...do you like it?"

"Hmmmm," I expressed with eyes wide open and looking around.

I saw a chair kept along-with a table with lots of sharpened HB pencils in yellow color lying in a pen stand and a bunch of chart papers. There was a table lamp and a drafter on that table. So, he must have been a professional architect or a student doing some design course.

"Oh it's getting hot, let's turn on the fan," he said as he made me sit on a small round stool.

"Do you have a pen?" I asked.

"Yes, lots of different colored pens."

"I use pencil to write and always wanted a pen, but my parents say that I would use pen only when I reach my 4th standard. But I want one now…"

"Oh, that is not a problem at all. I will give you whichever pen you like," saying this, the guy bolted the door and turned on his small Black & White TV set.

He took me in his lap and started kissing and touching me. I had no idea of what's going on.

"Wow, put your hand inside and keep it there…" as he pulled down his under pants and took my hands there. He got massages and many up and down motions.

After ten minutes, he was wet all over and looked at me with a smile.

"I'll come back in a moment," saying that he went into his washroom.

Then he gave me a blue pen and said, "I have to go now, let's play this game tomorrow again."

"But…I want to play with my toy cart."

"I will give you a red pen tomorrow and a lot of toffees if you come."

"Okay," I said as I moved out of his room without having any idea of what has happened.

I got downstairs and called upon Raju.

"Hey Raju, come here. See what I got?" I called him in loud voice.

Raju came running to me and said, "What?"

"See my new pen. Isn't it good? I will write and draw in pen now."

"Yes, it's good."

"How many holidays do you have in your school?"

"Till 31st March, the same as in your school."

"Okay," as I took hold of his hand and we sat on the steps of stairs.

"I am very afraid of dogs," I said.

"No, that is a very cute puppy. It does not bite," Raju said making a funny looking face.

I touched his bare feet and unconsciously brought his feet to my belly and felt some pleasure. We did not know what we were doing and why. This was the time when my first symptoms of *podophilia* appeared, which is a type of *paraphilia*, called *partialism*.

After this incident, that guy did the same thing on four to five occasions and asked me not to tell this to anyone like my parents or friends.

I also kept quiet.

* * *

Next day, my mother said to my father, "Look at my girl...how weak she has become. Whatever she eats, she takes it out without digesting. Her fever is going up and down. Let's show her to a good doctor today."

My superstitious father replied, "Oh well, it may be due to ill sight (*buri nazar*) of somebody and I should take her to the temple priest (*pandit ji*)."

Then, both started offering prayers to God in front of their pictures.

"Today, I'll have my duty swapped with a colleague and I will go to my factory at 2 pm, night shift," my father continued.

"Okay," as my mother started preparing for food.

My father took my mother and sister on his bicycle asking me to take care of myself and not to go anywhere.

I started playing with Raju.

"Let's play with puppy," Raju said as we went out of the main gate of the house.

"No, I am afraid of dogs," I said to Raju.

"Oh come on, nothing will happen," Raju raised his eyebrows now.

As we started rolling and tossing the small puppy, it bit me in my left leg and blood started coming out. I started crying, but Raju fled from the scene.

An aunt from neighborhood came and said, "Oh my God, that's dog bite and you are so small boy. There are fourteen injections that go into belly."

When my parents returned from temple after fifteen minutes or so, my mother started beating me, "I said that don't go anywhere. Why did you go out to play and now this dog bite? What should I do now?"

One of the aunt said, "Bite is very small and from a little puppy. Bring some red chili powder and turmeric powder to cure this superficial bite."

Powders were thrown on the dog bitten area and it caused a lot of pain. But after few days, I was fine without the need of getting any injections.

* * *

31st March 1984, 9 AM:

"Today we have to go to school and attend the prize distribution function to get the result card of our boy," my mother said to my father.

"I have to go to my colleague's home, so you must go to school with Rahul. I will take care of Ritu," my father replied and wow, now you know my sister's name too.

"Alright," as my mother took hold of my hand and we went to my school on foot. It just took five minutes to reach there as my school was nearby.

"After nursery, now the turn for K.G. class and the first position goes to Rahul," my Principal Madam made the announcement from her dais.

My mother smiled and I got on to the stage and received

my result card along with a notebook and pencil as prize. I jumped with joy.

Then I with my mother returned back home.

She advised me on the way, “Always read louder and it helps to memorize fast. You will do well in your higher classes by cramming tables.”

I was happy when my father padded my back that day.

❑

Two

I studied in a Hindi medium school located in the nearby residential area. Our Principal, popularly called '*Badey Madam*' (Big Boss) by teachers, was a very dominating and strict lady. To beat a student or two in a day for minor issues was normal for her.

Physique of Principal Madam was like a WWF champion and she used to wear *sari*. Teachers of my school were very hardworking and sincere.

In my 4th standard, I started to learn Punjabi — the regional language of our state also. I was good in drawing and teachers used to praise me in my class.

I was getting attracted to girls and from this age of mere 8 years, I started shagging almost daily for several times. Nothing came out, but it made me feeling happy. I was becoming addicted to it slowly but had no clue.

I had a binoculars gifted by my paternal uncle and I used it to watch girls' soft feet, who used to play in our street around my house.

One day, my mother caught me and broke my binoculars.

"Just study well and play less," my mother instructed me in stern voice.

I used to play hop-scotch with girls of my street. Don't know why, but girls also liked to play with me and did not talk much to other boys. May be because I was soft and polite due to my over controlling, aggressive and nagging parents.

More I used to study and bring good marks, more my parents seemed to be dissatisfied.

First time, I failed in Mathematics paper when I could just score 16 marks out of 100. I was given back my marked papers by the teacher to show these to parents and get their signatures.

That day, my father was already disturbed due to strike in his factory.

"You bloody dog, so less marks," as my father slapped hard on my face.

"Next time if you ever fail, I will throw you out of my house," father continued with a very aggressive look on his face.

My sister Ritu was terrified to show her papers. She scored less but was at least passing in all the subjects.

"Both of you listen to me carefully...if you do not want to toil hard as a worker in a company like me, study hard and you will make your life. If you do not study well, no one will ask you. Understood?"

I and Ritu both nodded silently.

My father used to give Mathematics problems to me

and my sister when he used to go to market and asked us to solve all questions till he returned back.

"Ok Rahul, your solutions are correct," my father said as he finished checking my notebook.

I felt a sigh of relief.

"And you Ritu, dumbo...why so many are wrong? Don't you understand what I taught you?" saying this father slapped her so hard that the impression of his five fingers was left on her cheek and she pissed off.

"Don't be so harsh with kids; they will slowly learn everything," my mother cried from kitchen.

"Okay, spoil the kids, I cannot feed them throughout my life," my father said and started to take rest on his bed.

My first century in the subject of Mathematics was in my 6th standard. Moreover, I also scored very well in other subjects.

Now I became the topper of my school and it made my parents feel proud.

My teachers were also very happy and they informed my parents to visit the school's Principal.

Next day, I came along with my father in Principal's office and he said to Principal, "Madam Ji, my son is very naughty. I bought him so many toys especially cars and helicopter, which he disassembles and spoils."

Principal replied with a big smile on her face, "Oh no, he is a very bright kid. I know we are strict, but he will shine one day because of his hard work and determination.

I saw he performed very well in this session. Keep it up dear Ashish. You see, one day your son will become an engineer if he disassembles his toys to see their internal functioning."

My class teacher was also sitting there for my feedback.

She said, "Only thing which irritates us most is that Rahul talks too much and asks so many questions that sometimes we are left with very little time for classroom teaching."

Principal interrupted and said, "Let him ask questions, its good."

My class teacher continued, "Her sister Ritu does not pay much attention to details. Please ask her to write at least ten words daily in her notebook to improve the vocabulary and especially her poor handwriting."

"Alright madam thanks a lot. I should leave now." saying this; my father left my school's gate.

Principal then came to my classroom and announced, "Look students, Rahul will be the class monitor from now onwards."

The previous class monitor felt jealous, but did not say anything to anyone and accepted the official order.

* * *

My sister Ritu was in 6th standard when I was going to be in 8th standard. My final exams for 7th standard had just finished in the month of February. I was the topper throughout and now everyone knew that I am the one who will bring laurels to that small school one day.

It was the festival of colors — *Holi*, in the month of March 1992. Now we had moved to our own home; a two bedroom flat on third floor.

I was hanging from my terrace wall and was throwing colored water balloons on people going on the road below.

I asked my sister to fill the barrel of my *pichkaari* that was brought by my maternal uncle last day, as both of us started to find kids to throw our colored water at them.

Suddenly, I got sight of a very beautiful young girl and I said with happy face, "Look Ritu, we got someone to play. Come on fast."

Ritu saw that girl and said, "Hey, she's Shalu; my classmate!"

I said, "Isn't she very cute and beautiful?"

"Yes, and she always stands first in my class."

"Excellent," I said as one topper meets and greets another topper.

I emptied my *pichkaari* fully on Shalu, when she looked upwards and smiled at me and my sister. Her fair face and beautiful hair were shining in the bright sunlight. I was literally mesmerized with my love at first sight experience. She's my first crush.

"Hi Shalu, how are you?" my sister yelled in loud voice.

"I am fine. Can we play today?" Shalu asked.

"Yes, but my mother does not like us to spoil our

clothes as some kids play really dirty in this festival. We will come to your home to play in the evening," my sister replied.

"That's perfectly fine. I will wait for you." Shalu replied as she left that place.

* * *

I along with my sister went to Shalu's flat located on ground floor of another street.

'Knock-knock' and Shalu opened the door with big smile on her face.

Shalu's little brother brought me a glass of water.

There was so much silence in their beautifully decorated home.

I asked, "Is there no one in your house?"

Shalu replied, "No, my parents have gone out to meet my uncle."

Ritu said, "Shalu, will you please show me your new makeup box?"

As both girls got engaged, Shalu's brother started showing me his drawing book.

"Shivam Sharma, your name?" I asked little boy after I read his name from the sticker on drawing book.

"Yes," little boy said in very shy manner.

"Wow, we are Sharmas too!" I said.

Shalu looked at me lovingly and I tried to hug her but she felt shy. Her face turned reddish as she blushed.

One boy came running and opened our door. He said, "Rahul, your father is calling you for study. Go fast as he is very angry."

I hurried to my house and then my father said, "Look son, you have board exams this year. If you keep playing like this and do not get good marks, you will not get admission in a good Government Model school of Chandigarh."

I started with my studies and Ritu returned back from Shalu's home after 15-20 minutes.

"*Bhaiya* (Brother), you know an aunt from the adjacent house had come to Shalu's room when you had left..." my sister said in breathless tone.

"Who was that aunt?" I asked in surprise.

"I don't know, but she was rebuking my friend Shalu. She strictly asked her to keep away from you as you are a bad boy. I think she was watching us play in Shalu's house from that open window of Shalu's drawing room." my sister continued.

"Oh...I see," I said with sad expression.

"That aunt also said if she ever saw you with Shalu, she would complain to our parents and Shalu's parents as well."

"My God, it's serious. If that ever happens, my father will throw me out of this house," I said with terrified look.

From that day, I took an oath to keep away from girls and concentrate on my studies only.

One day my father said, "Your Mathematics score is

fine but I want same hundred percent score in Science also."

"Ok daddy, I will try my best."

"No you are not going to try, you'll have to get. Science and Mathematics subjects will make your future. You know we are general category people and *Mandal commission* has announced reserved quota for SC/ST class and we are the people who would struggle hard for admissions and jobs now," my father said.

I could feel the pressure of middle class struggle for survival.

"You know I could not buy a color TV till now because I want you to study and get a good job," my father said.

"Okay," I said to close the conversation.

* * *

The students of 7th standard used to sit with students of my class in a combined room just adjacent to Principal Madam's room. Wooden benches were placed very closely as it was a small school. Students were creating noise as one of the teachers was absent that day. Principal then came to our room.

"Hey Rahul, just control your class. There are parents sitting in my office and you people are creating so much chaos. I want to have pin drop silence. Understood?" Principal said in stern voice.

"Sure madam," I said as I stood from my seat and came in front of the class.

Two of my bench mates were getting physically intimate with each other, and when I started to pull one to make them sit quietly, he got hold of my balls and I cried in pain.

I just sat on my seat and did not tell anyone about it.

Principal just came to our class again after ten minutes and adjusted the period with her English class. She made us perfect in English language with strong emphasis on grammar.

"Sorry buddy," the guy who had just hurt me started to massage on my groins area and said, "My name is Ashwani and I live near your street."

"No issues, we are friends now," I said with my tear filled eyes.

Ashwani wiped my tears with his handkerchief.

I smiled and just felt a sense of pleasure when he was rubbing his hands on my pants.

"Alright class, I want you to change all the sentences in your English workbook from Active to Passive voice and I want to see your homework tomorrow," Principal said in loud and commanding voice.

"Okay madam," our class replied in chorus.

That day, I went back to my home with Ashwani.

I bought some *papad* (round shaped appetizer) and gave some to Ashwani. He was very happy.

Ashwani's house was just on the way; located in front

of Shalu's house and her mother came out to open the door. I saw her briefly and then we said "Bye" to each other. She was in a bit angry mood.

Next day, I met Ashwani in my class and said, "Is your mother strict?"

"Yes dear, but my father is cool." Ashwani said.

"Oh it's just the opposite in my house. My mother is bit lenient but my father is very strict. Even my teachers say that he's overly strict."

I don't know what prompted him, but Ashwani kissed on my cheeks and said, "You are my dearest friend."

He used to touch me all the time and I too enjoyed it.

In recess time, he shared his lunch with me.

I met my sister on water tap and she said, "What are you doing with that boy?"

"Oh, Ashwani? He's my good friend. I used to play with girls and everyone made fun of me. I do not like loafer boys. Girls are sincere and they understand me well. But this is the first boy, who clicked with me so well," I said.

"Oh, really? I must tell you that he is the son of that aunt who came to meet Shalu that day and was responsible for your breakup with my best friend," Ritu said.

"But now, I cannot leave his friendship. He is very nice. What is his fault if his mother is like that?" I replied.

"Okay as you wish," saying this Ritu left for her class as the bell rang for next period.

* * *

Next day in class, Ashwani could not do his English homework and he was copying it from my notebook.

Suddenly, Principal came inside our classroom and announced, "Today, I will take two periods. Students, just open your notebooks and start with active-passive voice exercise that I gave you yesterday."

"Stand up Ashwani," Principal shouted.

Ashwani stood with shivering hands and said, "Madam, I could not do my homework."

I don't know what prompted my Principal that day that she poured away all her frustration on soft and slim hands of Ashwani. She used the side of a ruler and beat Ashwani mercilessly.

"You bloody donkey...you won't pass in board exams next year. Your English is already poor and you don't work hard. You will become laborer one day."

Ashwani felt sorry but nothing could stop fury of Principal that day.

His small hands were swollen and he kept weeping. Tears rolled out from my eyes also.

After Principal's class time was over, I took hold of Ashwani's hands and kissed them. I soothed him and said, "You can come to my home and I will help you in your homework."

"Okay buddy, thanks," Ashwani smiled.

We became very close friends but destiny ruled my life.

* * *

It was the month of December 1992 and I used to wake up at 5 am in the morning and sometimes 4 am to cram dates and events of my History subject. I also revised Science and Math formulas.

I became very busy as final board exams were nearby in the month of February, 1993.

I did very well in my board exams and the result of my U.T. Board middle standard examination was out in the month of April, 1993.

My father did not wait and I got easy admission in a good English medium school, because my past academic record was very good.

He got me admitted to a private school only as someone told him that Government model schools lacked discipline.

❑

Three

My high school was a big building with beautiful garden and a big playground although I never played any sports in my previous school because it only concentrated on study. Though it was a co-educational school, boys and girls were made to sit separately in different rows.

My father purchased me books for my 9th standard on the very first day of my school. My admission was confirmed as the result of my board exams was out. I had topped in Chandigarh with 3rd rank and got prize from my previous school's Principal and praises for being a merit holder.

The news spread like a wild fire and it impressed my teachers in new school also.

Now the expectations from me were even higher, but nobody had the idea of how difficult it was for me because of a change in medium of instructions from Hindi to English.

Everything was in English except that I took Social Science in Hindi medium. I could do well in Mathematics as my logic and concepts were clear, but I was facing some difficulty in Science subject. My English books in Course-A were also very hard to grasp.

One day an uncle came to my house and I said, "Uncle, I am having very hard time in studying the subject of Science in English medium."

"Just show me your textbook son," uncle said.

"Here, it is..."

"Oh God, that's the first chapter — Nature of Matter, and it is the simplest one. Your basics start from here; elements, compounds etc. Dear you have to still see the difficult part of subject, its easy one."

I was looking at uncle's face with surprise in my eyes wide open.

"What should I do now? I have almost given up!"

"Son, do one thing...use dictionary to see the meanings and write them in pencil on your book wherever you encounter a difficult word," uncle advised me.

"Yes, my daddy has taught me how to see meaning of a word in dictionary. He had taught me algebra in my junior classes and I still did not forget any formula."

"Excellent son! Best of Luck." saying this uncle took his tea and left my home.

* * *

As my new school was little away from my house, my father bought me a bicycle.

I worked very hard using the method that uncle

suggested me and within 3-4 months I got comfortable in English medium books.

One day, I asked the topper girl of my class, "Navneet, please show me your Science practical file, because I don't know about list of experiments. I could not come to the school yesterday due to fever."

"No no, I can't help you. My friend has taken my practical file," she replied in a totally refusal tone.

A boy named Vikram was monitor of our class and he was listening to my conversation with Navneet.

"Rahul, now you are the hope of boys of our class. Do very well in the forthcoming exams as you did in your board exams. These girls think they are very intelligent and we boys are nothing in front of them. I want to break the attitude of this girl," Vikram said.

"Sure, I will try my best."

My science teacher was very sincere and hardworking too. She never got irritated on my silly questions.

I got full marks in my first term Science paper and my teacher kissed me in front of students of my class. I felt very shy as she had left her red lipstick mark on my cheek.

All my teachers were very happy with my performance.

My class teacher said, "Students, just look at this boy. He's from a Hindi medium school and left each one of you so much behind in exams. You should be ashamed as you are already in English medium from beginning."

Navneet really got jealous as she used to come at first position and her marks were 100 less than mine in grand total of 600 marks.

Navneet asked me, "Rahul, please tell me your time table. What is the way you do your study?"

I said, "I have no special method that I follow for studies. Only the thing is that I am fully dedicated and give my heart and soul to whatever I do."

"Wow, you are cool."

"Thanks Navneet," and after this, she became my friend.

Principal of the school came to our class and she also appreciated me. She announced, "we will keep class monitor for this class (Vikram) unchanged. But I'm making Rahul, the Head Boy of the school."

Students of my class clapped and boys started shaking hands with me.

I became popular in my school.

* * *

It was summer time and we had vacations. I started to have itching in my hair.

Soon, I discovered a lot of dandruff in my hair and the problem increased in a few days.

I said to my father, "Daddy, I want to apply a good shampoo to my hair as there is a lot of dandruff. I can't use soap to wash my hair now."

"Why don't you use mustard oil?"

"Daddy, I even applied curd in my hair before I rinsed them in bathroom. Mother did not allow me to use eggs in my hair as we are Hindus. Please give me some money to buy shampoo sachets."

"I have no money for these useless and expensive cosmetic items."

"Okay," I said with sad expression as I now knew what a lower middle class upbringing means.

I remembered my childhood times when I used to play School-School with little kids. Just like a classroom teacher, I used to take their attendance and taught those tables. My sister used to play with dolls and Home-Home (*ghar-ghar*) game with her friend.

I asked my mother, "Mom, I want to start coaching."

"Oh, you are so intelligent. You are the school topper now, and not a weak student. Why do you need tuition classes?"

"No mom, I want to teach."

"Oh God, you are yourself a child...who would send his kids to you?"

"No mom, please ask that aunt. I mean that tailor who was telling you one day that someone needs coaching."

"Alright, I will ask her today evening when I go to her home to take my newly sewed suit."

"Ok," I said and felt very happy.

My mother returned from tailor and said, "Son, her husband's colleague is a Bengali and their family have come from Delhi. They need some good tutor for their only son, who is in 8th standard and studies in English medium under ICSE board. You are yourself in 9th standard. I don't know if they will agree. But your aunt says that she will talk to them and get back to us soon."

After two days, aunt's son came to my house to call me.

I went to aunt's flat and said, "*Namaste* (Hello) auntie."

Aunt said, "Oh Rahul, come inside."

I sat on their sofa and aunt's son brought me a glass of water.

"Did you talk to them?" I asked with hope.

"Oh yes, that's why I have called you. Vasu is a Bengali boy and a student of 8th standard, ICSE board. Their parents want a passionate tutor who can teach their son all the subjects like English, Mathematics and Science. But you have to go to their house to teach him. If you are fine, you can go from tomorrow," aunt explained to me in detail.

"Yes, that's fine with me. Please tell them I am going to teach Vasu from tomorrow. Thank you so much for your reference."

"My pleasure son, you deserve that as you are so hard working and sincere boy."

"Okay auntie ji, I must leave now."

"Best of luck."

After this, I came back to my home.

My mother asked, "So, what did she say?"

"Mom, I am going to teach Vasu from tomorrow. Their house is in phase-4 and I will go on my bicycle to teach him in his house," I said.

"Okay, but take care of your studies first as your father is very strict about your marks and grades."

"Don't worry mom, I will not give you any chance to complain."

"Okay, then I will talk to your father today," as my mother concluded.

My father allowed me to earn my first income from this coaching business.

Next day, I went to Vasu's home and rang their door bell.

'Ting-Tong' and Vasu's mother opened the door and said, "Oh Rahul, come inside."

I saw Vasu's house which was big and beautifully decorated.

"That is Vasu's study room. Please sit on that chair and I will call him. You can introduce yourself and I send you a glass of water in servant's hand," said Vasu's mother as she made me feel at home.

"That's fine with me," I replied.

"Vasu, get up from bed you lethargic boy. See your tutor has come," Vasu's mother called upon Vasu from other room.

Vasu came rubbing his eyes and was happy to see a young boy of his age group to teach him.

"Hi Vasu, my name is Rahul. I am your home tutor for all subjects."

"Wow, we will rock!"

"Sure dear, may I know your score in unit tests held recently?"

"Please don't ask as his marks are too low. He is not as intelligent as you are..." said Vasu's mother.

"No issues auntie, I just wanted to know where my student stands and what his weak areas are," I clarified.

"He used to score very well but when we came from Delhi due to change in workplace of my husband, Vasu is finding it difficult to adjust to new school. He managed to score just 17, 15 and 10 marks out of 30 in unit tests of English, Science and Mathematics respectively. Now, you need to help him," replied Vasu's mother.

"I will try my best," I assured her.

Vasu's mother respected me like a guru of her child and used to offer me a cup of tea with biscuits daily in my 2-hour class with Vasu.

I started taking chapter-wise tests to assess Vasu's understanding of whatever I taught him.

To my surprise and even greater surprise for Vasu's mother, Vasu scored 28, 29 and 30 marks in first test of English, Science and Mathematics.

She gave my payment of Rupees 400 and that was my first earning from my coaching business.

After being a good student, I could now say that I am a good teacher also.

With my first payment, I bought sweets for my parents and they were very happy to see their son doing so well on studies as well as teaching others.

Now, I had no need to ask my father for pocket money. I could buy my shampoo and other things I needed from my money. I tried many shampoos and at last, I got relief from H&S shampoo. Its pouch was costly. Other shampoos cost 50 paisa to 1 rupee and that sachet of H&S cost Rupees 3 in those times also. But it was very effective, so I bought even the expensive one.

Vasu showed the same results in his school tests and his parents were really happy with my teaching. They increased my payment from rupees 400 to 500 per month.

Final exams of 9th standard were over and I bagged the first position in my class. I kept teaching in parallel.

* * *

I used to take rounds in my school as part of my duty as Head boy of the school and made sure that kids come and leave in queue for morning assembly and follow discipline. Head girl — Kanchan, used to assist me, who was daughter of my Hindi teacher from my previous Hindi-medium school.

One day, I met my old love Ashwani, while going downstairs.

He said, "My friend Rahul, I have taken admission in your school."

"Wow, but this is school for rich people. We are poor guys. I don't know how my father is managing to pay my fees here."

"Anyways, it is indeed a pleasure to meet you after a long time."

"Same here, but now I have less time for your friendship as I am more focused in studies and earning part-time income from coaching as well."

We shook hands and then parted away. This was the first biggest mistake of my life...I was leaving love for need of money.

After doing well in his final exams, Vasu started coming to my home for tuition class and brought one of his class mates with him.

One day in school, I got attracted to a girl in 7th standard, whom I saw in morning assembly and while going through main corridor, she bumped in to me as she was running for her class on the first floor. I felt like heaven in her arms.

I told this incident to my best friend Vikas. He was son of rich dad but discouraged me to pursue girls as he was my well wisher too. He did not want teachers to know about this as it brings bad name to institution.

* * *

One fine morning, I was on my usual round. I met that girl along with her two friends; one girl from 8th standard and another from 9th standard. I changed my path; thinking that they may create a scene.

Next morning, the trio of these girls blocked my path

and one of the girls said, "Please listen to us Rahul, just for a minute..."

"Yes, tell me what do you want?"

"Why are you trying to avoid us? We have observed many times that every time we try to approach you and talk to you, you change your path which is absolutely awkward and insulting to us. We wanted to congratulate you for your grand success in final exams of 9th class. You did really well," the 9th class girl said in questioning tone.

"Did we ever say or do anything to hurt you?" the 8th class girl asked.

"Please tell us today. We want a reply from you", said the 7th class girl along with her friends.

I said assertively, "Hey girls you are getting me wrong. You have totally misunderstood me. I am not trying to avoid you, but I do not want any friendship with girls."

"Why so? Are we not beautiful enough? I am so fair and cute as my friends tell me," the 8th class girl said.

"No you are definitely very smart. I can only say one thing that there is a lot of status gap between us. You girls are from rich backgrounds and I am from a lower middle-class family. We don't have even a color TV. Remember that a king's son is a king and labor's son is always a laborer," I told my logic to pacify the girls.

"Hey come on...why do you think like that? Times change and may be you become richer than us one day," the 9th class girl said.

"I don't think that day will ever come. I am really sorry girls. I don't want to hurt your sentiments but please don't compel me."

"Okay, we won't approach you again. Take care." the girls said as they shook hands with me and left the place in low mood.

Refusing the love of these girls due to my financial position was the second biggest mistake of my life.

Boys of my class used to tease me for not making girl friends, but I did not pay much attention to them.

My sports instructor was very tough guy. He used to make students, who did not come in proper uniform, run for five rounds in playground.

One day, meeting of our school management trust was going on and I was in-charge of three classrooms.

My sports instructor came to our classroom and said, "Rahul whoever creates chaos in class, warn him once and write his name on the blackboard if he or she does not listen to you."

"Okay sir," I said.

Some disturbing elements were not cooperating with me and I wrote their names on blackboard. Sports instructor came and asked the defaulters to come out. He beat those boys with sticks and shoes and then asked them to run for several rounds of playground.

In afternoon, when school bell rang I came in parking area and to my surprise, my bicycle was missing. It was a big shock as my father would kill me if he comes to know that my bicycle has been stolen.

Luckily, my bicycle with broken lock was found lying beside the trunk of a tree. I felt a sense of relief and started heading back to my home as my strict parents wanted me to be in time everyday and not to go anywhere else.

On my way back home, some boys surrounded me and warned me of dire consequences if they ever got beaten up by the sports instructor again.

This was my first lesson to not become that much honest in politics and then, I started deviating from my Head boy duty. I started to focus more on my studies as I had my secondary board exams nearby.

* * *

One day my social science teacher was teaching a geography chapter. I was reading out the names of world's highest mountains like Mount Everest, Kanchanjunga, and then I said Nanga parvat while reading in a flow.

Whole class burst into fits of laughter.

Then that teacher stopped my reading in between and said, "Look at this hypocritical generation. All of you watch channels like Fashion TV, STAR Movies and MTV on your cable TV network and make fun of such a name for a mountain."

My class mate Aditya sitting besides me on the desk whispered in my ears, "Our teacher must be watching such channels also, that's why she knows these channels show *nange log* (nude people)."

I laughed at his punch. Then, Aditya asked me to come to his home and play video game after school.

I was very excited and went to his house in evening time.

There was no one in his house at that time. My friend Aditya served cold coffee to me while I sit in front of his big color TV set and Samurai TV game system. It had a game cartridge loaded into the slot and a laser gun attached. I enjoyed playing racing-car game with the joystick.

Aditya then opened an English magazine and showed me various models in nude and semi-nude postures.

"What is this?" I asked.

"Beautiful babe dude, don't you like her?" Aditya said.

"They are beautiful but sorry to say; I have no attraction for such things. I want to play one more game."

"Ok buddy as you wish."

I played and enjoyed another set of racing game.

Aditya started reading about an incident of a sexual encounter of a boy and girl in that magazine, "Look Rahul, it's interesting!"

"No, let me play dude, my last chance to win."

I was very happy to finish the game in first position and that night I could not sleep and just dreamed of owing my own video game system.

"How much is the cost of that game console?" I asked Aditya next day in my classroom.

"I don't know as my grandfather had gifted me on my

birthday. I think price is Rupees 3000-4000," Aditya replied.

"Oh that's so costly!"

"No problem buddy, I will get my hand-held video game and we can play in free period."

"Ok, thanks my dear friend."

I collected money from my coaching business and bought myself a TV game system within few months. Although not that costly as Aditya's, but it was good enough to play games likes Super Mario, Contra, Pac man, Bomber Man, Space Invaders etc. I spent Rupees 1500 on this system.

My parents objected to such a purchase and asked me to focus on my studies.

One day, an NGO visited in our school campus. They had a TV set and few brochures to circulate in students.

They called all the school girls separately for one hour sessions and taught them about the use of Whisper pads.

I had no idea about periods as my Science teacher was very shy to teach us the chapters of Human Reproduction.

Some of the boys in my class requested Principal Madam to attend the session, but she refused saying that there was nothing for boys in this.

I studied hard day and night. I again topped in my board exams and then I got an easy admission to a public school in Chandigarh as there were no higher secondary schools in Mohali at that time. I passed my matriculation exam in the year 1995.

❑

Four

I had got some free time after my class X examination. I got three kids of same family to teach in their house, which I could not continue for long time as I had a lot of pressure of my studies in the new school.

New school only offered PCM (non-medical) and PCB (medical) subjects. I had taken PCM subjects as I wanted to become an Engineer.

This school was one of the most sought after school in the region. Vice-Principal was a very strict lady and I was terrified to see that she used to beat even 12th standard boys over trivial issues anywhere anytime.

There were very few girls in our class as most girls were in PCB (Biology) section. My father wanted me to become a doctor and choose Biology in place of Mathematics.

One day, I saw 12th class girls doing dissection of a mouse in the Biology lab and it made me feel like vomiting. Then I saw two heavy books of Zoology and Botany lying beside on a table.

I told my father, "I can't do dissection as the sight of blood causes me mental pain. I should better become an engineer."

"Okay son, do as you wish," my father said in cheerful mood for first time in life as the biggest worry to get me admission in a Chandigarh school was now over.

* * *

I adapted very well to the environment of new school. I took Physical Education as optional subject.

I experienced my first ragging by my class mates only.

One boy asked me to read a poem after my introduction and other boy asked me to define the meaning of term 'sexy'?

I felt very shy and nervous at first. I answered in low tone, "Sexy is one who wears small clothes."

The group of boys standing there laughed loudly and one of them said, "You fool, Sec C is reciprocal of Cosine C."

I also laughed and made a few friends. Some of them were so open with me that they used to ask my shagging frequency. I was doing it 5-6 times daily.

I was taught Physics by Tayib Ali Khan in 11th class. He was doing PhD at that time and left my school for a job in Delhi University when I entered my 12th standard. He created my interest in the subject.

I never saw such a dedicated and passionate teacher in my life. He used to go to each student's desk and ask the numerical problems which students found difficult to solve.

I was made President (Boys) of this school by the

Principal Madam's order directly when I stood at the first position in my class (11th standard).

I became very popular in new school too and every class mate wanted my friendship. I used to be down to earth and easy going personality from very beginning due to the influence of parental values and religious ethics.

I used to feel closeness to few boys of my class as they used to hold my hand sometimes. We used to take a round of our school and playground in the free period.

I got the student bus pass issued from State Transport Authority for commuting from my place in Mohali to Chandigarh. The bus on my route was usually overcrowded and sometimes an unknown *Sardar* (a Sikh guy with beard and turban) used to molest me in the crowded bus.

After a few months, my father bought me a moped (2-wheeler) to save my travel time and avoid the inconvenience of crowded bus.

I used to study so hard throughout the day that I was not left with even a single minute for myself.

I used to solve all the unsolved exercise questions and numerical problems by myself in the subjects of Physics and Chemistry. My teachers used to avoid me sometimes so that I could not ask them my difficult problems.

One day, a cultural function was organized in our school.

All the students of my class were sitting in the assembly ground. My Principal addressed the crowd and welcomed the chief guest.

One of my class mate named Amar and a girl of 10th class named Shilpa were found kissing each other by my sports instructor through a small window opening of my classroom. They were sitting in close positions in the last seat, thinking that they were all alone.

Next day, the sports instructor told this incident to Vice-Principal Madam and she called Amar and Shilpa from their classrooms and openly slapped both of them multiple times in the middle of school campus.

She said, "Both of you listen to me carefully. Stop whatever you are doing...it's my school and such things are not allowed. You will defame the reputation of this school for which I spent years of hard work and dedication to bring it to this level. Next time, I will call your parents and throw you out of my school. Understand?"

"Yes madam," both Amar and Shilpa nodded in unison.

"Now go back to your classrooms," saying this she left the place.

I was now determined to never ever go near girls. I felt sorry for Amar and an aggressive feeling for overly strict Vice-Principal.

I topped my final exams again and passed my 12th board exams with flying colors in the year 1997.

Next challenge was to appear for several Engineering entrance exams and get admission in an engineering college.

I got very good ranks in diploma entrance tests as well as engineering exams because my concepts were very clear.

❑

Five

I with my father went to Jalandhar City of Punjab to attend the counseling for engineering colleges in University campus, which sprawled in multiple acres of land and appeared to me as a small town or city in itself.

I wanted to take Electronics and Communication / Instrumentation branch, but good institutes were getting full quickly as the number of seats in those times were very few.

Computer Science and Engineering was new field and my father asked me to choose that branch.

I agreed and we completed the admission formalities. My father paid the fees and it was 11 pm in the night that the things could reach some conclusion.

I selected a local college for myself, which was newly opened as the first college of our area. I did not want to leave mother and my parents too did not want me to live a hostel life away from home.

I was happy as mine would be the first batch and I would be saved from ragging.

* * *

My college was outside the city limits and located in a village area that was peaceful and full of greenery.

My first time experience of this developing college was awesome.

First, I missed the college sight as there was no gate, but just a small patch of rough road from a small gate post located near main road.

There were six rooms (three on either side) of this under construction building where just one office and two labs were built in addition to three classrooms or lecture halls. Literally, there was no library and only a computer lab was there which contained just 15-20 Intel 486 PCs in very bad state.

There was a small hut in the name of canteen where students used to struggle to get a piece of meal.

Ours was a class of 60 students with only 6 girl students.

I started giving coaching for engineering diploma entrance test in my flat as well as teaching engineering Mathematics. I became a popular tutor in my area.

I worked hard day and night and bagged first position in my class and good University grades.

My college teachers used to praise me as an ideal and most favorite student.

I could not perform my practical work due to old and insufficient number of PCs that were available in computer lab for 60 students of our class.

My father borrowed money from his company and bought me a Pentium grade brand new PC for home practice. Its cost was around Rupees 50,000 at that time.

I used to help my classmates by providing my notebook and practical files. I had to work on their part also when in a project group, but I also learnt many things.

One night at 10 pm, one boy came to my house and said, "Rahul please help me."

"Who are you? I never saw you in my class."

Boy was bit shocked to hear this, but said, "I am Honey... I mean Harpreet Singh Sidhu. You are an intelligent guy and sit in front seat. I am a back bencher. I need your notes otherwise I am going to fail in the University exam tomorrow."

"Don't worry my friend. You can take my notebook and I will read from book."

"Thanks a lot. Good night."

One day, some jealous students stole my notebook and that time nobody came to my rescue. I was the one who helped whole class and now I realized that I really got no real friend in my degree time. All the needy fellows just used me. However, I topped in all the semesters, year after year.

Despite the initial difficulties of a developing infrastructure, lack of books and experienced staff, lack of laboratory equipments, I gave my best to my engineering degree and passed out in the year 2001 scoring 4th rank in entire state. I had topped in the University merit list.

My college came in lime light and my name was written on the honors board.

This was the first biggest achievement of my life.

* * *

There were no campus placements as it was a new college and IT sector went into severe economic recession triggered by dot-com blast in the year 2001.

One of my classmates suffered severe depression because of no job opportunity and had to be admitted in hospital.

It was very tough time when we had no jobs in market.

I started to work in an institute as senior faculty as they were looking for just diploma pass-outs. I just left the job as it was clerical and the institute did not make my salary payment in time.

Then, I started to work as a faculty in University contact centers and as a Web Developer in a small company in Chandigarh, only when I happened to meet a South Indian guy in the office of that small company.

I asked, "Hi, what are you doing here?"

"Dude I am looking for a job. You know these turbulent times... I was Team Leader in a medium scale company in Bangalore earning Rupees 50,000 per month and now coming to Chandigarh to find a job. You know when my company had shut the operations of my department and offered a job of Rupees 5000 per month, I had to quit.

Can you imagine a fall to one-tenth?" replied the black South Indian guy.

"Oh, that's really sad state of affairs. Please have some patience. Everything will be alright." I consoled him.

Teaching had turned out to be my core passion from just a childhood hobby. As compared to job, I was making good money in part-time coaching business and used to save most of my money in bank.

I learnt a lot while working as Web Developer, but after 5-6 months, I was asked to see some other job as the market condition was very bad and my company was not getting any project work.

As I already had the idea of this expulsion, I had started working in a computer institute in Sector-34 Chandigarh side by side.

❑

Six

I was selected as faculty when I presented my strong Resume and impressed the MD of the Institute with my communication and presentation skills.

I joined this institute in September 2001. It was a distance education center of some University and used to run various computer courses like part time M.Sc. (IT) etc.

Catch was that I was not given any appointment letter.

I used to get up at 5 am in the morning and prepare for my lecture. After taking my breakfast, I used to leave my home at 6.30 am and reached the institute to take my theory and practical classes from 7 am to 10:30 am. Students were also working as employees somewhere and clicked very well with me.

After these morning classes, I used to do my second job of Web developer from 11 am to 4:30 pm. Then, I used to come back to institute at 5 pm for part time evening classes and returned back to my home at 11pm at night after finishing my last class at 10:30 pm. So, I was working 15-16 hours per day.

Everything seemed to be fine for a hardworking and sincere guy as me, but my first payment for month of September was delayed till October end and the cheque that institute gave to me, got bounced.

I approached institute's Head called Deepali and said, "Look madam the cheque you have given to me is returned back from your bank due to insufficient funds. I am working hard day and night. Please clear my payment."

"No problem, please return the cheque and we'll make you cash payment," Deepali replied.

In the end of October month, I was paid the salary in cash. I thought everything is alright now, but never knew that this was nothing new for the institute as they used to make payments to faculty via cheque, which got bounced most of the time. Institute's MD used to scare people away without making their payments such that they had to leave job, but I had no idea of all this.

Salary for the month of October was again given to me in the form of a cheque for Rupees 6000 in the mid of November month. As expected, this cheque also got bounced.

I approached madam Deepali and said, "Now the second cheque has been dishonored. What is going on?"

Deepali said, "Oh Rahul, I will ask MD about it. See this is business and it is just a coincidence that it happened with you second time. I really feel sorry. We normally make cheque from our current account and sometimes the cheque gets returned due to insufficient funds."

"When will the MD come to institute?"

"He is out of station and I will talk to him as soon as he comes."

"Alright."

"Please have patience; no body will keep your money."

"Thanks," saying that I went to take my classes after signing their attendance register kept near stairs as usual.

One day I met that cheap MD of the institute in his office. He said, "We have some payments due from our students. It's not only you, but nobody in the institute has received their October month salary. We will make your payment maximum by December end. Please bear with us."

"I will work till November end as I am looking for a new job now."

"Okay as you wish."

I kept in touch with institute after leaving that job and kept requesting them to make my payment.

Institute issued another cheque for Rupees 6000 with a date of mid January 2002, assuring to me that the cheque will clear my payment this time. MD said, "We shall make cash payment for your October month in the meantime and then you can please present this cheque in your bank to clear your November month's salary."

"Okay thank you sir." I said and came out of the institute.

To my utter surprise, neither I got any cash payment nor was the cheque cleared. It was stopped.

I rushed to institute and asked Deepali, "What is going

on? Why are you harassing me? Please make my payments that are due. I already visited your institute so many times."

Deepali said, "You can talk to MD sir, I don't know."

"What the hell? Where is he?"

"He is busy in some meeting. Come tomorrow."

"Wow, what a joke... you guys have no intention to make my payments."

"Just leave my office or I will complain and ask security to show you the door."

"Yes, I am going now and will come back with police."

"No problem, you can go anywhere. MD sir is experienced in such things. You can not do anything, try whatever you like," Deepali said in aggressive tone throwing a challenge on me.

I first approached sector-34 police-station with a copy of my bounced cheque, but they started threatening me and asked me to settle the case myself with institute. But I had already tried to settle several times.

I hired an advocate and spent around 1000 rupees to send UPC of legal notices to institute, which they returned back saying that there were no such persons in institute.

Advocate asked so much money that I could not proceed with the case.

I approached a newspaper to help me, but they did not entertain me. Why would they? They were not getting anything from me by supporting the cause or truth. They are business minded and earned from advertisements of institutes, mainly from sector-34, Chandigarh.

Someone told me that it was a case of fraud and I should report in Economic Offense Wing (EWO) located in sector-17, Chandigarh.

I filed a complaint with Chandigarh police from Public window system, but it also did not help either. Someone told me that EOW does not deal with such petty amounts. But Rupees 12,000 in dishonored cheques; was a big amount for me.

I had no option but to file a case myself in *Lok Adalat* (public trial court) which started in the court of the Chief Judicial Magistrate (CJM).

In February 2002, I had joined a government institute, where people were nice and helped me learn many things. I was a faculty in training department but I had to leave as it was a contractual job of 6 months.

I happened to visit my college and talked to my Dean Academics, who advised me to join the college as Lecturer in place of getting such treatment by rogue people in the market. She knew I am a good, innocent and sincere guy and that is why I was being cheated by people easily.

I along with my father kept on visiting *Lok Adalat* in sector-9 and then district courts in sector-17 of Chandigarh, for our case hearing for more than 1 ½ years, but the corrupt judge did not do anything. I spent all my casual leaves from my new college job in fighting this case, but in vain.

One fine day, CJM's reader said to us, "Your case should be filed in labor court and we can not help much."

I did not say anything and came to know why MD had no fear of the system. He had nexus with bank managers, sector-34 police and now he must have given bribe to this judge also.

I thought it's to better leave the case and let this fucking system go to hell. I wasted about two years in the process in addition to mental harassment and wastage of money.

❑

Seven

Going back to the same college to teach where I was once a student was an extra-ordinary experience.

Some people were comfortable, while others were not that much happy to see me as lecturer at their level because of ego.

I worked hard with full sincerity as usual and didn't face much difficulty.

My father along-with some help from my side, purchased a plot in a residential colony on the outskirts of Chandigarh. We had sold our flat and now moved to a house as tenants again.

It took a struggle and hard work of one and a half year to build our house. It was the second biggest achievement of my life that I got experience of building my house from foundation to finishing.

One day my Head of Department said, "Rahul, now you have a good home also, you should get married."

"Yes madam, my parents are already trying through newspaper..."

"Oh God, you have to marry; not your parents. I think you better try yourself."

"Thanks for the advice. I think you are right."

"You are idealistic like your parents and people make a fool out of you. You are hard working but now-a-days smart work is more important Rahul."

"Sure," saying this I left her office.

I came back home and said to my mother, "Mom, I am 23 years old and now in lecturer-ship from past one year."

"Right, but what are you trying to say?" my mother asked.

"When will I get married?"

My mother smiled and said, "We are trying to find a match for you, but *pandit ji* (priest) says that you will get married only after 29 years of age."

"What? Why so late?"

"Oh son, you are *manglik* and the girl's horoscope should match with yours and she must be *manglik* too."

"What the hell...what will happen if I get married to a *non-manglik* girl?"

"Then one of the spouses may die after marriage. We have witnessed such incidents in our extended family. I don't want to lose you son. You are our only son and support of our life."

"Okay mom, I will advertise for a *manglik* match in newspaper."

"Son, your father is of dominating nature and he has not many friends in his company. Moreover, no relative as such is telling us any suitable match. So, you have to try on our own."

"Alright."

After spending a sum of 5000 rupees in different English dailies, one day I got a phone call from mother of a girl.

"Hello, I want to talk regarding your matrimonial advertisement," the lady on other side of phone said.

"Who are you and is your girl *manglik*?"

"Yes, she is *manglik* and I am girl's mother."

"Okay, I am the boy who advertised in newspaper and willing to marry."

"Son, can I talk to any elder person in your family like your mother?"

"Sorry, nobody is present in my home right now. You can talk to me."

"Okay son, what are you doing?"

"I am working as Lecturer in Computer Science department of an engineering college. I had topped in the University, so they have given me a job there only."

"That's fine, but how much is your salary son?"

"I am getting Rupees 9800 per month as starting pay and will get a raise soon."

"Sorry," saying that the lady disconnected the telephone signaling to me that she wanted a higher pay package guy not an ordinary lecturer like me.

I started feeling low as I had no girl friends because of my focus in studies and this marriage thing was getting to my nerves.

I bought paid memberships of various matrimonial websites, but did not get proper response because the expectations of middle-class people were very high.

One day, my Head of Department said to me, "So Rahul, any progress?"

"No madam."

"Why so? You are good looking and now in a job."

"But madam, I am *manglik* and after we find a horoscope match, people do not entertain us properly. I tried to contact people who give advertisements, but some want doctors, IAS etc and others want an NRI match or an IIT/IIM pass out at least. Do I have any hope?"

"Yes, people these days give more importance to status and money in place of a compatible and loving match. It's because of globalization of our economy and IT MNCs that have made people more greedy and materialistic. You are very talented and young by age. Why don't you try in industry?"

"Madam, I would love to go to industry. But the times of year 2001 still scare me when industry was passing from severe recession. In teaching field, recession does not have that much impact. I don't know what to do?"

"But my dear student and now my teacher, the teaching field does not offer much growth. All you will get is Rs 400 increment per year and see where the inflation is going...petrol now costs Rupees 58 a litre which was Rupees

32 a litre two years ago. To live a happy life, money is vital. I suggest that you pursue higher studies from some renowned college or University and try to get selected in campus placements that you missed in this college."

"Okay, thank you so much for the advice. But don't you think I am late for such a change? What will happen if industry faces a recession again?"

"*Jab jago tabhi savera* (You are never late). I think industry will now stabilize. If good times are not permanent, bad times are also not permanent. Give a try at least."

"Sure I will. Thanks."

I left my job after completing two years and got admission for Master degree course in very reputed college of Chandigarh.

One day, my father said to me, "Son, don't expect any help from my side. I have to save for your sister's marriage and I have no more money left for your education. I have already spent all my money in building the house and have to repay the housing loans too."

I assured my father, "Daddy I will do part time coaching as I was doing before and I will take care of all the expenses. You need not give even a single penny."

My father sighed with relief.

* * *

One day a lady called me regarding matrimonial advertisement.

"Hello, I saw your matrimonial advertisement in a matrimonial website."

"Yes, I am the boy but I am *manglik.*"

"Oh that's good, my daughter is *manglik* too. What are you doing son?"

"I am working as a Lecturer in a college and now took a break to pursue higher studies. What is your girl's qualification?"

"Oh, she has just completed her graduation and now doing part time B.Ed. What is your future plan?"

"I am confident to get a company job and a good pay package if selected by a good company in campus placements drive."

"Your college is reputed, but I am sorry you are not settled in your life. We want a match who is stable and earning."

"But madam your daughter is also not doing anything..."

"That's none of your business," and lady disconnected the call.

I thought that lady wanted someone who is settled with a wife and having kids too...what a joke! *Manglik* girls even aged more than me were waiting for their perfect match but not taking the marriage alliance seriously. Everyone was talking as if it's a business deal not a life partner search.

* * *

It was my final semester. My written test was clear in 2-3 companies and I got at interview stage in one MNC.

Technical interview, group discussion all went fine and the last was HR round, where the interview panel asked me few questions.

"Mr. Rahul, did you sleep well last night?"

"Yes, its part of life. I was already prepared for interview."

"Okay solve this puzzle for me," he handled me a paper and passed on a ball pen.

In place of taking his pen, I took mine from shirt pocket and solved the puzzle.

"Impressive, I like that you came with your own pen. Otherwise, people forget to take small things with them like a pen."

"You have a gap of more than two years in pursuing your education and you first adopted teaching field. Some companies do not even allow such candidates to sit in the test," another guy tried to incite me.

"Sir, there was no such criteria mentioned by you and I do not regret doing something in place of sitting idle at my home."

"Okay, give us few reasons why we should hire you?" the HR head asked me.

"I have given my best for selection and the same performance I would deliver in my job. If you still do not hire me, you are the loser, I am not," I said.

"Wow! What a confidence man. We have selected you. Best of luck for your future! Please take your offer letter and report to our Noida office on the date mentioned there."

Person shook hands with me and I said with smiling face, "Thank you sir."

* * *

My parents were overwhelmed with joy and my father said, "Son, now our dreams are going to be fulfilled. You have got the job in your field and no more teaching. Go to company and make your future."

"Yes daddy. Here are sweets for you. Mom, you also take."

"No son, we should first go to temple and worship our God and pray for your bright future."

"Still I am lagging in marriage part mom."

"Oh, marriages are made in heaven. Don't worry; you will get a good match."

The phone bell rang as my mother finished saying that.

"Hello, I am from Amritsar and want to talk about the matrimonial alliance of our daughter with your son."

"Yes madam. I am the boy."

"No no, I want to talk to your mother or father."

"Mom, take the call for my matrimonial," I said as I passed phone to her.

"Let daddy talk to her as I am washing clothes."

My father said, "Yes madam."

"I saw your matrimonial advertisement in website and my daughter liked particulars of your boy. She is *manglik* and just completed her M. Sc. What is your son doing?"

"He has got a break in industry and left his teaching job. He will complete his Masters degree by this May month and join an MNC in Noida."

"That's great. We would like to meet you with family. I will inform you when my husband comes back from office in the evening."

"Okay madam, thanks. We shall wait for your call."

My father made the call when we did not receive their call by 10 pm at night.

"Hello, we had a chat in day time regarding matrimonial alliance of my son with your daughter."

"Oh yes, I was about to call you. My wife just told me that you had a conversation," the girl's father replied on call.

"So, what is your plan?"

"Let's meet this Saturday in Sukhna Lake at 5 pm and then we can discuss in details."

"Sure sir. I also want boy and girl to meet each other first," my father replied.

My parents along with me and my sister hired an auto-rickshaw and reached Sukhna Lake at exact time. We waited for their call and it was 5:30 pm.

Now the clock was at 6 pm and I said, "Daddy, call them and ask why they did not turn up till now?"

My father called girl's father, "Hello sir, we have reached Sukhna Lake at the decided time and we were waiting for you."

"We won't be coming today. Let's meet some other time." girl's father replied.

"Why? What happened?"

"My daughter has gone for an interview so she is not available."

"Sir, we came as per the place and time decided by you. If you had a change of plan then at least you should have told us."

"You sticky fellow, we have informed you now, okay?" saying this girl's father disconnected the call.

"What the hell these fucking bastards think of themselves. People say I am dominating and these bloody sick people showing this cheap attitude. They had called us and insulted us without reason," my father said in frustration.

"Don't worry daddy, maybe I deserve better," I consoled.

After this, we all came back home.

* * *

My father kept trying very hard and after few days, one more call came.

"Hello," the person on call said.

"Hello, yes sir," my father replied.

"You had called us few days back for matrimonial alliance. We have matched the horoscope of your boy with our girl. If you want, let's proceed to make your boy meet our girl."

"Sure sir, when are you coming to meet us?"

"Can't you come to us in Ludhiana? It's not that far."

"Distance is not a problem sir, but I am not well these days and my wife is not used to go out all alone."

"Okay, then we can come to your home this Sunday."

"Most welcome sir."

As the whole day of Sunday passed and there was no intimation from girl's side, my father called the girl's father.

"Hello sir, you were supposed to meet us today. Are you coming or not?"

"Sorry, we can't come."

"Why so?"

"Actually, our *beybey* (an elderly lady) says that boys come to see girls and not the other way round. We really respect her and she also says that the day is not auspicious to meet," girl's father replied.

"Oh really, then you should have fixed the meeting after taking her permission. Sir, times have changed and you are still having so orthodox views and talking in a conservative way. We are also religious and believe in horoscope matching, but don't have so much ego that only other party has to come and we can't come to meet," my father said in loud voice.

"Stop it, it's our wish that we want to come or not. Who are you to dictate us?"

"I am not dictating anything. Why are you putting unnecessary terms and conditions to meet? Selecting a right match is not a joke. Either you listen to the old lady or support growth based progressive thinking."

"No, we don't want now. You don't know how to speak to others."

"Okay, then get lost," saying this my father disconnected the call in angry mood.

I said, "Daddy if we were very rich like a businessman or an industrialist, girls would have come in a queue to marry me. You need not take any stress. I don't want relation with such families who can not respect my parents. You have worked day and night and made so many sacrifices to make my life successful."

My father said with tired face, "I don't know why the luck of my child is so bad that nobody is taking the marriage seriously."

"Leave these morons. We won't give up dad and definitely find a better match one day."

❑

Eight

It was the month of May, 2006 and I passed my Masters degree in distinction. Now the time was near when I was about to leave my parent's home and start a new job and a new life in a new place. I attended the convocation function of my college and got my Masters Degree certificate.

In the month of July 2006, I went to New Delhi by train as company had sponsored 2nd class AC fare. I was accompanied by two more guys from Chandigarh. We introduced each other and were seated in the same coach. My sister gifted me a mobile phone, while I was leaving home for first time in my life.

After getting down in Delhi, we hired a cab and reported to the Noida office of the company as per details in our offer letter.

Company's head office was beautiful as I saw the big glass building with a lush green garden and fountains. I took instant coffee from the vending machine on entering the reception premises.

We were asked to keep our luggage at the main gate and were made to sit in a big auditorium hall.

A company official directed us, "We welcome you all to join our company. Hope you are doing well. Your induction training for 10 days will be held in a college in Greater Noida. Our buses will take you there and you will live in their hostel. So, all of you are required to maintain proper discipline there. Company will provide you three meals a day and attendance is mandatory for all the presentations that our experts would take in college auditorium. So, all of you get ready to go and watch a movie in the meantime so we make necessary arrangements."

* * *

I was going with my luggage in company bus on the Greater Noida expressway. I got down at college campus and I was told to share the room in hostel with two guys from Kolkata, West Bengal.

On the very first day, company got the forms filled and we were required to sign a 1 ½ year contract with them. All of us signed the documents and completed the formalities.

I asked an official, "When would you pay for our train ticket? I have kept it safe."

He behaved in very casual way and said, "HR department said that we can't make the payment as all the candidates have not preserved their travel tickets because they did not know of the compensation. So, we have decided to not pay anyone as it would create partiality. Moreover, to pay any amount we would need proof; that many guys don't have unlike you."

I tore my train ticket and thought that it might be a fair cause.

Company focused on presentations on various topics like goal setting, teamwork, communication skills, leadership etc and we did some interesting activities. It was a good learning experience.

Company showed us various inspiring movies, some of them I remember were: *Man of Horror, October sky, Traveling Birds* and *Remember the Titans*.

I was made to watch my first porn movie in college hostel by some guys there.

Slowly, I became good friends with those Bengali guys. I had good impression about Bengali people from very beginning as I taught Vasu in 8th standard.

On last day of our induction training, our HR manager addressed us and said, "There are no shortcuts to success and if there are any, please don't follow them. You will realize that your hard-work and perseverance pays in the end. I have instructions to send guys from North to company's offices in South and vice-versa. But your batch will remain in Northern state. On my end, if you want to choose your job location, let me know. Your choice is between Gurgaon and Noida. But I am making you this favor on your request; so please do not talk about this outside this room."

All of us were very happy that we're free to choose our place of work.

Somebody told me that Noida was not a safe area as there were a lot of crimes there and many areas were under development. Frankly speaking, even I did not like the place as I was comparing it to Chandigarh.

However, I had to make a quick decision. I had seen Panchkula in Haryana and thought that Gurgaon may be similar. One girl came to me and said, "Rahul, I had got posting in Gurgaon and my home is in Noida. I don't want to leave my parents. You are outsider so it hardly matters for where you join. Can you exchange my Gurgaon posting with your Noida posting?"

"Yes, sure," I said with smiling face as that's what I was also looking for.

My Bengali friends also got posting in the same place - Gurgaon.

After making my HR manager note of our preference of job location, I asked, "Would company make any arrangement for our stay as I have nobody to support me in this region and this is the first time I will go to Gurgaon?"

"Company has a guest house where you can stay, but it's very expensive. Better will be that you take some hotel room and then search for a room on rent or PG (Paying Guest) accommodation with the help of classified ads or property dealers of that area," HR manager replied.

I with those two Bengali friends hired a cab and we took a hotel room in Sector-4, Gurgaon for our initial stay.

On a weekend, we started our search for a house and through a property consultant; we went to see a house of a Colonel in Sector-23.

It was a three-room set on ground floor of a very big house, which Colonel wanted to rent out. House was spacious but finishing work was still going on. Walls were in poor condition as the old house was not maintained properly. Colonel's family used to live on first floor with little luggage as if they lived somewhere else.

I said to my Bengali friend, "Abhishek; isn't this accommodation a bit big for us? We could manage well in smaller space."

Abhishek said, "We don't have many options as property dealer says that only a few houses are available on rent here. We can not be in a hotel room for long time as it's expensive."

I said, "Colonel Sir, what will be the rent for this accommodation?"

Colonel replied, "I told Rupees 10,000 per month to your dealer but on his request that you have newly joined office here, I would charge Rupees 9,000 per month but you have to deposit 2 months rent as advance."

I whispered to Abhishek, "Its too high rent. Should we not look for other option like PG accommodation?"

"I liked the spacious rooms with attached washrooms and I am ready to pay Rupees 9000 to book this accommodation now." Abhishek said.

"Okay sir, we are ready but when will the finishing work conclude?"

"Oh you need not worry at all. Just shift in one room with your luggage while the finishing work is complete for other rooms, then you can swap to get your room finalized. Work should be complete in 10 odd days," Colonel replied.

Dealer said, "So sir, you can take Rupees 9000 now and they will pay other Rupees 9000 in 2-3 days time while we make the rent agreement papers."

Abhishek asked while giving money to Colonel, "Sir, can we shift in the house tomorrow as we are staying in a hotel room now?"

Colonel said laughingly, "Oh you desperate soul, you are most welcome. You can shift tomorrow only. Only seven more days of this month are left."

We bought bed mattress and other necessary items and shifted in Colonel's house.

Next day, I paid second part payment to Colonel and said, "Sir, we have paid you the full security amount now."

"That's right. You can see the Lease Agreement that I just got from your property dealer."

I saw that the date for paying the monthly rental was 7th of each English calendar month.

"Okay sir, please complete the formalities and we sign the papers," I said. There was a reason to trust here because the property dealer we hired was from a reference of the local relative of Abhishek. But we never knew that Colonel was a rogue person.

He went to property dealer and got the payment date changed from 7th to 1st of every month, when we were in office for work.

When I just read the papers before signing, I said, "Sir, we have newly joined our company and company has still to open our salary accounts. My HR manager says that our first salary will be through cheque although I will try for some advance cash payment, but it's not fair to change the earlier date to first of each month. Please give us some time to make the rent payment of our first month."

Property dealer did not utter a single word and Colonel went back to his jeep in angry mood as we did not sign the Lease Agreement.

Dealer stood up from the seat in his office and hurriedly went to the Colonel's jeep and said, "I feel sorry for their behavior. Please forgive them as they are kids. I will get the papers signed tomorrow."

"Okay," Colonel said in rude tone.

Next day, property dealer came to Colonel's house and my friends and Colonel was also there.

I said to dealer, "See we three guys are living here in one shared room for past ten days and still we have not got full possession of the place we are paying for. Finishing work may not complete before the end of this month."

Colonel said, "I had given you shelter in my house and your friend was desperate to live here. I did not call you to live here."

I said, "Sir we have already paid you the advance security amount as you asked. You should also fulfill your commitment to first give us full possession."

Colonel said, "I did not like the way you speak. It's my house and if you do not like then, you can vacate from here."

Abhishek said, "Sorry sir we did not mean that. All we need is time to adjust here. Last night rain came inside the room because of the broken window panes. My friend Abhi from Kolkata got sick, because of the stress of payments which I am taking care for him."

Colonel said mockingly, "That's not my concern and you can ask to your dealer. I am not directly dealing with you. I never promised that you will get mineral water to drink in my house."

Property dealer left the place in sad expression.

Before we could say anything, Colonel asked us to pay the rent amount by first of month or vacate the place now as he has other tenant waiting.

Abhi's mother came all the way from Kolkata via train as she was worried to see her son. She was told on phone by Abhishek that her son was sick.

Colonel asked, "I am very particular about my payment. So are you making the payment now or vacating the house?"

Abhishek said, "Sir, my friend's mother is coming from Kolkata. She would stay for a night here and then go back tomorrow. We would vacate your house as soon as we get an accommodation this weekend or by tomorrow."

"I don't care for your friend's mother. You can go to hell along with her. I want my house to be vacated now," Colonel said in insensitive and selfish tone.

I could not believe how a person of such a high rank and responsible post can behave in such a way. It was a shock when he forced us out of his house in the evening only.

I along with Abhishek started looking for a room and suddenly we saw in nearby market an advertisement for a PG accommodation.

I talked to the contact person on phone and we made a shift to that PG room that night only. Abhi's mother also took back her son to Kolkata and commented on Colonel with bad words.

* * *

We got a nice room in PG and property dealer got our second payment back from Colonel, which I and Abhishek divided equally. Colonel had charged us whopping Rupees 9000 for just 10 day stay in his house.

PG accommodation was full of people from different states and mostly the guys were students, doing MBA as their college was nearby that building.

Boys were very friendly to me but not that much to Abhishek. It may be because of my easy going nature as I am a Libran.

Most of the boys used to drink and smoke but they never forced me to join them.

PG owner took his payment from me and assured us of comfortable stay.

Food that was served was full of chilies so that consumption remained least possible — all businesses work that way. Cooks used to run away as PG owner did not make their payments. I was reminded of my times in that institute which paid me with cheque that got bounced.

However, the company paid my first salary in time and to my surprise my pay package was equated to candidates with Bachelors degree.

Next day, I approached my HR manager and said, "Look at my offer letter and my yearly pay package is Rupees 20,000 more than what you have given to Bachelor candidates. I have done Masters Degree."

"Oh don't you worry. It may be mistake of payroll department because in your group you are the only exception," my HR manager replied.

The issue was settled as I got the difference in next month's salary. I could not make out why nobody in this city is fair enough in their dealings?

* * *

I used to wake up early in the morning but there was always a big queue in the shared washroom of that PG. Abhishek could not cope up with oily food of PG and this wait time and took a room on rent in another house having a Bengali landlord.

One day, I was going to my office in *Udyog Vihar* (Industrial Area). I took an auto-rickshaw as usual. There was only one guy who got down in the mid way.

When I just got down for office, I could not find my mobile phone. Before I could talk to driver, he had gone.

I did not know what to do. There was a marching crowd of laborers and if I got into that it would be difficult for me to find out where I dropped my phone.

Most probably, phone had slipped from my pocket due to that bumpy road or that guy sitting beside me; must have stolen it.

I tried to call my phone number from my colleague's phone, who was going to office on the way, but my phone was switched off.

Without wasting any time, I took an auto-rickshaw and tried to locate the auto-rickshaw that I came in. It was a stretch of 10 miles from auto-rickshaw stand near Gurgaon bus stand to my office and I looked through more than 200 auto-rickshaws and found the one I was traveling in just one hour.

I said to the driver, "I was in your auto-rickshaw and lost my mobile phone. Do you have it? Please give it to me."

"No boss, I don't have it," driver said.

"It was a gift from my sister. Please give to me; I will give you some money."

"I am telling the truth, the guy may have pick pocketed your cell phone. I have no idea. Sorry."

"Okay."

I had to file an FIR and stop the post paid (pay-monthly) phone connection by calling to my phone company.

* * *

After two months, I changed to a new PG accommodation, but the food remained a problem again.

That PG's owner was a property dealer and sometimes he used to misbehave with me as he used to come in drunken state at night. I did not like such guys.

One day, I chatted with Abhishek when he said, "Come on and live with me my friend if you wish. This landlord is good."

I bought few more household goods and shifted to his place as he had a spare room for me. Sharing that way reduced his rental cost to half and we were more comfortable and secure in a group.

Abhishek started to exploit my generosity. He did not share the household work and I had to manage things on my own.

He became a very lethargic and careless person.

One day he said, "Rahul, I had some money left openly near TV set and now I am finding that there are Rupees 10 less. Have you taken?"

I was in a shocked state as I never touched his things. I said, "Are you out of your mind? Why don't you keep your money in wallet and other important things in safe and locked place? Cook comes to your room and may be he has taken. I am not a thief to take your money. I would ask you if I need any money."

"I leave things open as I trusted you and *Tapan Da* (cook) can not take my money like that. He is a good guy."

"And I am bad, right? Okay, I will soon see a room for myself and you can live alone as before. You always share when you have to spend and when I have to spend or do some work, you sit back and relax."

"Yes, it's my room and I allowed you to live here."

"Okay, thanks for your kindness. I am leaving your room next month."

"Okay," Abhishek said.

* * *

I took a room at very high rent and shifted my belongings there. Landlord was from Jalandhar, Punjab and their house was located near market in Sector-22 of Gurgaon.

I managed everything very well as full control of my life was now in my hands. I was not dependent on anyone and got some peace of mind.

❑

Nine

Things were going smoothly in my office as my team was very cooperative and we had an experienced Project Manager and an enthusiastic Team Leader. Both were very strong technically and had onsite experience also.

I was assessed in *outstanding* performance band for two consecutive years. I clicked very well with Team Leader, who was from Bombay. He introduced me to project fully, guided me for Technical certification and provided his due support as and when I needed for on-the-job training.

Project Manager, who was an old guy from Delhi, was just promoted to senior level as he cleared his PMP certification.

Ours was a small team of eight members and we were on maintenance cum re-engineering project. We were providing support to a UK-based client.

One day our Business Unit (BU) head had a squabble with my team leader. Then he resigned from our company and joined another company in Bombay. It was a big shock for our team as we got de-motivated.

Project Manager had to bear more executive responsibilities now as no one in the team could yet be promoted to Team Leader level.

He kept requesting to BU head that he be transferred to another office of company else he would also resign from present job.

Some of the experienced guys from my team joined other projects in company's other offices. Obviously, pressure was now very high on new joiners like me.

BU head and my Project Manager both got transferred to company's Chennai office. At this time, a SPM (Senior Project Manager) who was a lady from other ailing project in our office was appointed as our new Project Manager.

Company was downsizing and focusing on cost cutting measures as Rupee fell in value compared to Dollar. Other companies also started crying over losses they were incurring. It had a direct impact on our salary raise.

Whenever I faced a tense moment, I used to shag in company's washroom.

* * *

One night, my mother said on phone, "Son when are you coming home?"

I replied, "Mom this weekend only."

"Good, we have talked to someone for your matrimonial alliance and the girl's parents wanted to come and meet you."

"That's good. I would meet them."

When I reached home and waited for girl's parents and nobody turned up, I asked my mother, "Mom, can you give me the contact number of these assholes? What do they think of themselves? Meeting time was 2 pm and its 6 pm now. It's Sunday and I will go back to office tomorrow. Why people make us wait unnecessarily?"

My mother said, "Okay let me call girl's mother."

"Hello, you did not turn up today. What happened?" my mother asked.

"Oh, I am in a car now. Your voice is not clear.... what are you saying?" the lady on other end replied.

"I am Rahul's mother and you were supposed to meet my son today. He may not take off from office again and is now available."

"Oh yes, I am really sorry. We went to see two more boys in Chandigarh and got late. Now we have reached Ambala city and going back to Delhi. If you wish to meet, we can wait for half an hour and you can meet us here."

"We don't have a car and you should have informed us at least. Moreover, it's not possible to reach Ambala in just 30 minutes."

"Okay, let's meet next time."

I took phone set from my mother and said, "That's so kind of you, but we are not that free for you. If you think marriage is a joke, then sell your daughter somewhere else. Get lost."

Lady disconnected the phone as expected.

Now the water was above my head and I literally lost interest in getting married.

I said to my mother, "Mom, if people are behaving like this before marriage then what will happen after marriage. I am thinking to adopt a child instead and it will help both of us. My life will find a meaning and the child's future will also be good with a caring and sincere guy as me."

Mother instantly replied, "Are you crazy? You are not going to adopt any orphan. I want to be grandmother of your natural baby. We can not trust that orphan as we don't know his/her background. We are trying our best to find a match for you. Have some patience, you will get one soon."

"Okay mom, as you say."

* * *

I started feeling low. That day, I got attracted to a teen boy named Sagar as I was roaming around my home and after a brief chat, we became very good friends.

I used to meet him whenever I visited my hometown. He used to live near my house in next-to-next street.

Sagar was crazy for songs, movies, video games etc and I had a big collection of such things to share with him.

Slowly he started coming to my bedroom. My parents objected but I denied listening to them.

We used to roam around and one day I caught his hand and said, "Dear Sagar, I think I am falling in love with you."

He hurriedly withdrew his hand and left that place without saying anything.

I thought he's not comfortable with me, so I parted my ways.

Still, I used to come that far every fortnight from Delhi to Chandigarh, just to see his glimpse. He was also observing me for long time. One day, he came with his friend and held my hand in the park to accept my proposal.

I was mad that day that I got love of my life. Slowly, I became possessive and obsessive for him. We used to exchange love SMSs but sometimes he used to behave in strange ways.

One day, I asked him, "Please tell me if you don't want me."

"No you are so good, I like you," Sagar replied.

I kissed him and made him sit in my lap as love and care is naturally present in my blood.

Sometimes, I felt like he was emotionally blackmailing me and using me. He did not love me in reality, but kept telling me lies that he loved me.

Sagar came to my house one night at 10 pm and said, "*Bhayia* (brother), my father needs a software urgently. Can you write a CD (Compact Disc) for me?"

I was taking my dinner at that time, but left my food for Sagar. I first gave him the CD he wanted.

Next day on Sunday, Sagar came and said, "My father is struggling with his Internet connection. Can you help him fix the issue?"

"Okay I will try. What happened?" I asked.

"My computer is not working properly and I wanted to play a video game."

"Sure love, my PC (Personal Computer) is all yours. You can play till you like."

Sagar was very happy to play the game and he got back one CD from his home to write that game.

To my surprise, that blank looking CD had an adult movie that played back on my PC.

"Oh, what is that?" Sagar asked.

"Go and return back this CD to your father and I'll give you this game in a new blank CD. I have a few spare blank CDs."

"Okay, thanks a lot brother."

Sagar ran back to his home and when I called him, he did not turn up on the given time. I felt broken and used.

I met Sagar's mother and she said, "Come inside son."

"Where is your PC?"

"There it is..." as she pointed to her husband sitting on a computer chair.

I fixed the Internet connection issue and Sagar's father said, "Thank you sir. Would you like to take some tea?"

"You are most welcome. I need to go back home now, so tea may be next time."

"Okay," as Sagar's father left me till the gate of his house.

When I came back to my hometown next time, I saw a big change in Sagar's behavior. He was not giving me proper attention and then I asked, "Sagar, give me my Software CD that I gave you last time."

Sagar was playing with his group of friends and kept ignoring me.

"Sagar, what happened to you? Tell me."

"Nothing, I have kept your CD safe. I will return it to you in 2-3 days."

I did not know that he was after girls and thus had no time for me.

When I did not get my CD returned till Sunday evening and I was to go back to my office on Monday, I approached Sagar's mother in her home.

"Auntie Ji, Sagar has taken my software CD and did not return back in time. I need some software urgently for my PC."

Sagar's mother replied in aggressive tone, "Sagar will give back your CD by 8 pm today. I will ask him what his problem was."

"No, please don't scold him."

I came back to my home and when Sagar came to return my CD, he said in angry tone, "Can't you wait? I was not going to eat your CD."

I was shocked and said, "Sagar that's not fair. Whenever you asked for any help I gave my best to fulfill it. Now I needed the CD and you failed to return back in time. You know I have to go back to my office tomorrow. I have to catch my bus for Delhi at 4 am in morning."

"Can't you take leave?" Sagar said.

"Oh dear, I can sacrifice myself for our love. It's not a matter of taking a leave but being sincere and fulfill your promise."

"I did not make any promise."

I was shaken from inside, but I ignored his behavior as I loved him.

That night, I visited a cybercafé for Internet and there I saw Sagar playing video game with the cybercafé owner, who was a young guy.

Sagar was holding his hand in front of me and made me feel jealous. I tried to speak to Sagar and when ignored I broke the CD that he had just returned to me in angry mood.

I could not take such an insult and ignorance to my love.

Next time when I came back my home, I visited Sagar's mother again.

I said, "I don't know why Sagar is ignoring me. When he came into my life the first time and left me on his own will, I was not hurt. This time he came into my life on his own will and then started ignoring me like this..."

"Dear Rahul, you both are like my sons. You know few days back when Sagar's father said something to him in loud voice in front of his friends, he did not speak to his father for many days. We have to tackle teenagers carefully else they may go on wrong path. You are a mature guy; therefore your understanding with Sagar will be bit difficult due to your age gap with him."

Listening to this conversation, Sagar's father came out of his room and started to speak in aggressive voice, "What happened?"

Sagar's mother replied, "Oh nothing serious…he's just feeling hurt as Sagar is not speaking to him properly."

Sagar's father said to me, "Sagar is just a kid and friendship is a relation of heart. Understand him or leave him."

"Sorry to disturb you, I am going back sir," I said.

I came back from their house with heavy heart. Nobody knew what I was going through. I was helpless as I had given away my heart to their son and they also had the idea of my love.

Next time, I came to know that some boys were telling Sagar that he's my Boy Friend. Historically, our society has never accepted love, so my case was not nothing new.

* * *

When I reached back my office, my SPM called me to see her in the meeting room.

She said, "Rahul we have seen your job performance and you have been *outstanding* for past two years. I have to select next person for onsite opportunity. Previous

Project Manager has recommended your name. So are you interested if we send you to London?"

"Yes madam, I am interested. Are you going to call back Ravi; the present onsite coordinator."

"Of course, as we have a small team and we send each of our team members on rotational basis. Let me discuss with your HR manager and new BU head that you are ready to go."

"Alright madam thanks."

"You have to understand all the project applications well so that you can provide live support to client's production system. We will give you 2 months to get prepared," she said.

"Okay madam."

I went to work with renewed energy and enthusiasm.

* * *

At night, I got a call from my mother and she said, "Good news son, we have talked to a girl's parents through their newspaper advertisement and they are visiting to meet us next time you come back home."

"What's the name of that girl and where are they from?"

"Name of the girl is Samriti and they are from Jalandhar, Punjab."

"Okay mom, Good night."

I met the girl and her parents in Chandigarh at Sukhna Lake.

I said to girl's father, "I like your daughter sir. Can I speak to her?"

"Yes son, why not? You can go on a walk with her and you can discuss and know about each other."

"So Samriti, I am Rahul."

"Yes I know and have seen your photograph also."

"So, do you like me?"

Samriti replied in a shy expression, "I am okay, but I would let my loving father take final decision for my match."

Then, I went to her father and asked, "Do you accept me sir?"

"Yes dear, it's yes from my side. I saw that you are an educated guy so I feel that you will do something in your life. My daughter will be happy with you."

"Thank you so much."

"Why don't you come to lunch in our house next time you come back?"

"Sure sir, we shall come to your house."

"Just call us when you reach there so that we receive you from main road and then we would take you to our home. Now we take your leave."

* * *

I went to my office and my SPM called me.

"So Rahul, keep your passport ready and fill out the UK visa forms. Start attending video conferencing sessions with client so that you can know each other well. We can find and fulfill the gaps, if any."

"Alright madam."

After few days, company's immigration department informed us that I have to get my passport reissued, because my educational certificates carried my middle name while my passport carried last name. UK government is very particular on such things.

It took a struggle of two months to get my passport reissued from Chandigarh.

"Rahul tell me if you are really interested to go to London or I find someone else to go?" my SPM called and asked me one day.

"Madam I will definitely go. What's my fault if the government process took that much time?"

"Don't argue with me. Ravi is an experienced and senior team member that I can not afford to lose after so many employees have already left our team. He is putting pressure on me for coming back."

"Why? What is the problem?"

"Ravi has to undergo some dental surgery. He is not able to concentrate on his job. Moreover, dental operation is very expensive in the UK. So, he wants to come back to his hometown and then his family can take care of him."

"Alright madam, please initiate the onsite transfer process. Now there will not be any delay from my side."

SPM smiled and said, “Okay.”

* * *

Next weekend, when I came back to my home, I along with my family visited Samriti’s house in Jalandhar.

Her parents treated us very nicely. But Samriti’s younger brother was constantly staring at me and made me think that he did not like me.

Samriti was sitting on a rotating computer chair in a relaxed mood and was watching her nail paint.

I asked her, “Do you know cooking?”

Samriti smiled and said, “Yes, but I do not cook much as you can see we have maids for our household work.”

“So are you ready to marry me?”

“Hmmm,” she bore a shy expression.

Samriti’s maternal aunt from other room asked my sister, “Your brother is very intelligent and working in a big MNC. Will he get well with Samriti? I mean does he want his way always or listens to others also?”

My sister said, “As far as I know my brother is caring and sensitive. But yes, he is bit assertive and likes to lead others.”

I said, “Auntie Ji, I am in an MNC and want the marriage to be concluded within a week as my office won’t give me ample time for this.”

Aunt said, “Oh that’s no problem. You are a good match for Samriti. We have to spend more money to get things done in small period of time, but we are ready for this."

"Thanks," I said.

Then, Samriti's maternal uncle asked me, "Son, what are your future plans?"

I said, "Uncle Ji, I have been working in this company for past two years and got promoted to the position of Lead Engineer. Now, my company is sending me to UK by the end of this month."

"Oh then; what about Samriti? Are you going to leave her in India only?"

"Oh sir, onsite opportunity is for one year and as per company's HR policy I can take my spouse with me if the stay is for more than 6 months."

"We trust you son. But just after marriage, you will go. How will you manage your relation?"

"Please don't worry. She would live with my parents in my house in Chandigarh. I am not going forever. I will come back. If you want, should I talk to my Project Manager just now?"

"Yes please."

I called my SPM and said with speakerphone on, "Hello madam."

"Yes Rahul?"

"Madam, my parents were trying for my marriage for many years and now we have found a match in Jalandhar. Girl's parents wanted me to assure them I would take her along to London. What is the process?"

"Look Rahul, we are already late in our proceedings and the client is waiting for you. Next week your work visa will come and then you would be required to catch your flight."

"But madam we found this *manglik* match after a lot of struggle and I am turning 28 this year. Our talks are in final stage and they are also ready for a quick marriage. Please tell me if I can take her along with me?"

"Project cost is already a concern for me and now you are asking me all this at the last moment?"

"Madam, I would bear her expenses. Company need not support her."

"Rahul think for a moment. Your new passport would not carry your spouse name. Company can give you letter, but it would depend upon UK Visa authority to grant her dependant visa. I can not assure anything. All I can promise is to give you break for marriage later when you adjust in the new place and job."

"How much break is possible?"

"I can give you even two months break for your marriage, when you come back. You won't be on Indian payroll when you are transferred to onsite location."

"Okay madam, thanks," and I disconnected the phone in sad mood.

Uncle said, "Son, I am sorry we can not proceed in that case."

My mother interrupted, "We can do engagement at least. In the meantime boy and girl could better know about each other."

Uncle said, "We are also trying to find her a match for long time. If we engaged her like this, then who knows your son gets a better option after UK return and then Samriti's marriage would remain on hold till your son is back. We might also lose other options."

My mother said, "Okay, we can't compel you. All we can do is to wait for my son's return and if Samriti is still single, we will proceed from where we left today."

"Yes, that's perfectly fine. Thanks for visiting us," uncle concluded.

"We liked you and your family," Samriti's father expressed in thankful posture.

"Same here," my father replied to girl's father and we left their house.

On our way home, I asked my mother, "Mom, would I ever get married?"

Mother said, "Oh son, come on. Now you are going to UK and there will be a queue of girls wanting to marry you. My neighbor says you will earn so much in one year that you will not earn in India in 5 years. It is a golden opportunity that you should not let go for marriage."

But how to explain her that I have my physical needs also. I never had any girl friend throughout my life. I kept silent as it would make no difference to her.

* * *

Next day, when I reached my office I could not focus well on work.

SPM came to my desk and said, “Rahul, either you marry and settle here or you go to London. You have to choose one...”

“I am going to London madam,” I said with heavy voice.

“Then, don’t blame me later.”

“Okay.”

“While you are at onsite, your parents can keep searching for a girl.”

“When should I send my belongings to Chandigarh? I need a day or two to make final settlements in my present house and then pack my luggage for London.”

“Formalities are complete and now you have to go with your documents to UK VFS center in Nehru Place, Delhi.”

“Okay madam.”

When I reached the UK immigration office, they asked me to get my photographs clicked again as they were very strict regarding the size. After this, they took my biometric retinal and fingerprint scans.

I got my work visa after 3-4 days. Company’s travel desk sent me Air tickets. My flight was scheduled on 27th September, 2008 via AirIndia’s Economy Class seat. Flight was from IGI airport in New Delhi to London’s Heathrow airport.

Company provided me Citibank card and some cash in the UK currency, which they deducted later in installments from my UK salary.

I hired Movers and Packers to transfer my belongings overnight from Gurgaon to Chandigarh, paying double charges.

When I came back to my home, I packed my luggage for London. I wanted some CDs to be written to DVD as I lacked space. So, I gave these CDs to that Cybercafé owner and asked the guy to give back the CDs same day as I was to go back.

Sagar was playing video games in that shop and smiled at me.

I said, "Sagar, I am going to London."

Sagar said with indifference, "then?"

"Hey I love you and you are behaving like we are strangers," I said.

"Okay, when will you come back?"

"After a year," I said, "I got a birthday gift and a greeting card for you, please take it from my home."

"But my birthday is in October, that is, next month."

"Oh darling, then I won't be in India. I wanted to give you in advance."

Cybercafé owner was Sagar's friend and he got jealous with my closeness and romantic behavior for Sagar.

He played smart and tried to close his shop in advance at night only when I reached and asked, "Hey, have you written DVDs for me?"

"I was busy in my shop and there were frequent electricity cuts."

"Oh God, it was urgent. If you could not complete the

given task, then you should have informed me and I had taken back my CDs."

"Now, come tomorrow. I have to go urgently."

"Oh dear it's just a matter of 2 minutes to re-open your shop and give me the CDs. I am going abroad, please don't hang me on."

I got back my CDs but he said in an aggressive tone, "You can not make someone love you like this."

I was shocked and surprised at the same time. I left his shop. Somewhere, Sagar was also responsible for all this drama.

Next day, I reached IGI airport, New Delhi and my parents had come to see me off. There were tears in my mother's eyes and I hugged her.

I kept on waiting for Sagar's call, but there was neither any call nor any message.

I called Sagar, "Hello Sagar?"

"Yes"

"You don't have any time for me. What is your problem? You know that I love you more than myself..." I started crying due to his ignorance, without knowing that he was after a girl who was his classmate in his school.

"But I don't love you."

I was in deep shock and said, "Then, why you kept telling me lies that you loved me for past one year? Did I not love you enough? Where did I lack? Please tell me…"

"I don't know. Don't disturb me. Go away."

❑

Ten

It was time to leave India and I entered the queue for security check. Verification process took around one hour and I was seated in AirIndia's plane. It was my first time that I sat in an aero-plane. My flight was at 1.45 am as per IST and the journey time was about 9 hours.

When the flight staff was telling about the emergency landing procedures and masks, I got to know the risks associated with air travel.

"We welcome you on-board. Plane is about to take off. Please fasten your seat belts and don't make sharp movements. Thanks!" the announcer said.

I just remembered the name of God and saw from window that how things on ground started to appear smaller and smaller as the plane took off from ground. Lights on ATC (Air Traffic Controller) tower and the runway slowly disappeared. I thought that I would get some weightless feeling as we have in a swing or lift going downwards, but it was nothing like that.

Plane seats were almost empty and there was no one

in business class also. I thought how the government is managing to run these planes economically.

When our plane reached to a stable height, it was silent and boring. It appeared as if plane is not moving at all and is standing there only.

Flight staff was very cordial. One air hostess dressed in *sari* - the typical AirIndia dress code, came to me and said, "Sir, we have many vacant seats. If you want to sleep use three seats in the middle row. Here is your blanket. Wish you a happy journey."

"Thank you so much. Where is washroom by the way?"

"Sir, please go on to the back side of plane."

"Okay thanks."

"Welcome," and the lady went away.

I saw how washroom had all the facilities in such a small space. Design of plane was really mind blowing.

I slept for some time and when I got up, just looked outside the window.

It was a marvelous sight. Our plane was flying much above clouds and the sun was shining across them; a very beautiful view indeed.

"We are reaching London's Heathrow airport in a few minutes from now. Please wear your seat belts." the announcer said.

I saw it was drizzling and the weather was cold. It was a beautiful sight to see England from above. All houses were of same color and size and mostly cars were parked outside those houses. Everything down there appeared so clean and well managed unlike India. Train tracks and roads were not overcrowded.

When I got down from plane, it was 7 am as per UK time. I could not locate my luggage on conveyor belt. I did not know what to do and where to complain about it.

I enquired from the AirIndia office there and my luggage came after an hour. I felt big relief.

I saw a text machine, some vending machines and currency converters.

I wanted to contact Ravi, but had not got any change for putting into public telephone.

I joined the queue for security checks. One UK border official asked me, "Gentleman, can I see your X-ray report?"

"Sorry sir, my X-ray scan was not done at New Delhi."

"Then, get your medical examination slip and wait there."

A lady dressed as nurse came from a room on opposite side and called people one by one.

A big fatty but fair lady on counter said in stern voice, "Oh you, why doesn't your government get your scan done before sending you here? It's our tax payer's money that we are spending for you."

I was shocked to hear all this, but replied patiently, "So sorry madam, I did not know that my X-ray report would be required here."

"Alright, take your slip and sit there for your turn."

I was taken to a room in front of a machine and was asked to remove my clothes. Then, the nurse got my chest X-ray scan and the report was okay.

I dressed up and came out of the room. It was Sunday and the airport was overly crowded as the flights from various countries had reached London.

Then I was to stand in long queues for various verification checks. It took me around six long hours to get out of the Heathrow airport.

On the exit gate, Ravi was already waiting for me.

"Welcome Rahul."

"Sorry Ravi, you had to wait for me for so long."

"It's fine. Let's go home now." saying this Ravi picked up my luggage and called a Black cab/taxi.

"Where sir?" driver asked.

"24, Kinch Grove, Preston Road," Ravi replied.

"Sure" and we reached Ravi's place in 15-20 minutes.

"How much mate?" Ravi asked.

"Four pounds and 50 pence darling," driver said.

Ravi made the payment as I had no change.

* * *

Neat and clean surroundings had already impressed me. There were no stray dogs on roads unlike India, no pollution and no dangling lose connections of electricity wires as we see in India.

Ravi was living with three South Indian guys in a shared house. House was hut shaped and big enough with water heaters and lawn area at backyard. Except one guy, South Indians could converse well in Hindi.

One of them was on student visa and used to go out in the night for newspaper sorting job. I could see in real how difficult it was to survive for students there.

"No doubt, we are getting so many good facilities in this developed country, but the cost of living is very high, mainly the items like accommodation and travel are quite expensive." Ravi said to me.

Next day, I got up early to go to client's office in time.

Ravi helped me to make my tube pass and get a new prepaid phone connection after few days. We boarded the tube from Wembley and got down in Central London. Platform lights were on in day time even. I thought this country has so much surplus electricity and my poor country lacks electricity.

I saw big buildings around, which were as high as 40 storeys and constructed with glass and steel. Red colored double Decker buses were going on roads. There were CCTV cameras everywhere and people were so civilized and rule following.

What surprised me most is that pedestrians were given time to cross the road and every vehicle used to wait for them even after their green signal was on. It was just opposite of India, where bigger and costlier vehicle owners never wait for others to cross the road.

I just crossed London's museum and saw an under

bridge where black granite stone was used lavishly all over and even the ceilings, where no body ever noticed. Wow this country is so rich, I thought.

The wooden benches were as old as 60s and those were unpainted but still in good condition. In England, weather is so nice and in India, we have to paint the iron benches and they get rusted soon. Throughout my stay in London, I never saw anyone watering plants as mild rains are a daily normal routine.

We entered a glass building and took a lift to my client's office on 9th floor.

Ravi introduced me to all British guys there. They too welcomed me very well.

Office was huge open area with BLOOMBERG TVs hanging all around. It was a financial company dealing in share trading and rating companies in the stock market.

Jack Smith was the person with whom I was to interact with on daily basis. Thomas Wilson was the technical consultant, a contractor who was hired by my client's company to get the work done from my company. We used to sit together for weekly video conferencing calls to our offshore project team in India.

Ravi sat with me all the day and slowly transferred all the system from his control to my control in a couple of days.

We went out for lunch. Ravi ordered a baked potato with Tuna sauce. I asked, "Ravi, isn't that a non-vegetarian food?"

"Yes Rahul, you have to take such food only. For

vegetarian food, either you have to cook it yourself or buy it at high cost."

One day, I found an Indian restaurant that offered vegetarian food. I spent about £ 7 on lunch which was costly and not even good enough.

I made myself fully flexible and it was the first time I started eating non-vegetarian. Once I ate meat balls with rice, I started eating whatever was available there.

We were back after lunch. Jack Smith said to Ravi, "Take Rahul to some strip clubs in London."

Ravi said, "Jack, he is not such type of guy."

"Oh, all work and no play will make Jack bore," Jack said smiling.

Jack asked me, "So, Rahul how did you find this place?"

I said, "Nice and beautiful city. Your country is very well managed, neat and clean."

"Great you liked. But how do you compare it to India?" Jack said in sarcastic tone expecting that I too like other Indians would start complaining about Indian systems.

To his surprise, I changed my tone and said, "Look Jack, I am an Indian and my heart is in India. I am here for work. Whatever you say to me is fine, but please never say anything against my culture, people and country in general."

Jack was bit annoyed but happy to listen such an answer. He shook hands with me and said, "Bravo mate, have a great stay here."

Ravi also left after a few days and said, “Best of luck Rahul. Now we’ll meet in India hopefully.”

Thomas Wilson had thrown a farewell party for Ravi. It was in a nearby hotel.

Ravi took a big glass of beer. Jack also offered me a mug of beer and then Ravi interrupted, “Sorry Jack, he does not drink.”

“What? Rahul does not drink. Strange mate,” Jack said.

“I will take coffee if you don’t mind,” I said.

“Oh yes, it’s okay mate,” Jack said.

* * *

After Ravi, now I was all alone to satisfy my client and meet his requirements like provide live support to their systems.

More I worked well, more work I used to get. Slowly Jack offloaded his responsibilities on me. For example, his task of writing MoM (Minutes of Meeting) was assigned to me.

Jack was a clerical guy and knew little bit technical stuff also. He used to send email for meetings by writing it again and again, taking about 20 minutes in the process.

One day he was not feeling well and asked me to send the mail. I did that in 5 minutes and next time, only in 2 minutes.

“Wicked,” Jack’s mouth was wide open in sheer

surprise when he saw the same task getting done by me in one tenth of the time he used to take.

I explained, "See Jack most of the time content and recipients of this email remain the same. So I created an email template, where I only change the date, time and venue of meeting. Contact list of recipients is picked up and then I simply click the Send button. That's it!"

"Terrific mate. You are genius," Jack said.

Similarly, I streamlined and optimized many such tasks. Client was very happy with my work. But British people kept on increasing their expectations from me.

Thomas Wilson also assigned me some of the responsibilities of their IT Manager as he once said to my SPM, "Rahul is technically very strong guy. He is doing well, but we will still take some time to fully rely on him."

Five days a week, I got busy like hell.

Jack started asking more favors from me like teaching his colleagues certain things which I knew could make their work easier.

He wanted my friendship desperately, but I did not fully give into Jack as I was not comfortable with his bullying nature, drinking habit and sometimes sarcastic behavior.

On weekends, I used to wash my clothes, prepare food and take rest. After few months, I started to feel like I am living a mechanical life.

I used to shag many times in office washroom to keep my physical stress level under control.

As per company's onsite documents, I was supposed to register with a doctor (called GP in London) in my local surgery. Client did not give me enough time to do the same for long time although I took a leave or two for banking work.

Our SPM was working like a puppet in the hands of my client as if she was desperate to not lose this account. She wanted to show our company that she could make an ailing project turn to profitable one. But how? Obviously, by sucking the blood of poor Indians like me.

One day, I went to James who was having some problem in the software. He was the most cheerful guy in client's office, whom I always saw with a smiling face.

Just when I was looking at his PC, he asked me, "Rahul have you got any girl friend in India?"

I said, "No James."

"Why so? Are you a gay?" he asked with smiling face.

I felt very shy and he just held my hand and said, "Sorry mate. I should not have asked you like that."

"It's okay. See your problem is fixed. Please give me a call if you face such problem again," I responded in a very formal way.

"Sure Rahul and thanks a lot."

Slowly, I got very good rapport with all the people in client's office. They used to respect me a lot. Believe it or not, Director of that company sometimes used to open door for me and say to me, "Good Morning sir. Would you like some coffee?"

It was like a dream to be at such a place with so nice people around.

I had purchased a laptop and used the Wi-Fi Internet connection at home. Internet speed was so high (10 Mbps to 50 Mbps) that it appeared to work like on local PC. Streaming videos were so fast as well as live TV channels.

I never saw any electricity cut or water problems. All the facilities were available 24X7.

It was the month of February 2009, when there was extreme snow fall in London. It broke a record of 200 years. Layer of snow on roads was more than 1 foot thick. Bus service got severely impacted. Not only London's tube was halted but also the UK government announced to close Heathrow airport operations for 3 days.

My SPM called me for the first time and said, "Hello Rahul, how are you doing?"

"I am fine madam. But we have a lot of snowfall here. I don't know if I would be able to go to office today. Buses and tube are not running."

"Look Rahul, we are in service industry. So, our project work and client is our first priority. Take your job seriously."

"That I agree madam. I will try to go to office but can not guarantee anything as the weather here is too bad."

"Jack will tell you alternate bus routes or you can take a cab. I will compensate your travel as per company rules."

"Okay madam."

I tried to take bus where stations were heavily overcrowded and after two hours I had to come back home.

SPM again called me, "Rahul why did you not report to client's office. Your presence was important as their business is important for our business."

I replied with cough, "But madam, I am having a fever as I caught cold."

"Oh God, I don't know anything. Company is suffering a loss of £ 150 per day if you don't go to client's office. Our project is already suffering from company's cost cutting measures and now this thing?"

"Madam, it's very inhumane of you to talk about money when my health is not fine. You talk about *Employee First* philosophy and now you are only talking about client."

"Behave yourself Rahul. I am the boss, don't teach me."

"Okay madam sorry."

Thomas Wilson had asked SPM to ensure uninterrupted and high quality services as they were paying well to my company.

In next video conference, Jack suggested, "Rahul should be given office laptop so that he can work from home in case of emergency."

But the cunning client never gave me any laptop and expected my laptop to be used for official work.

I started reading HR policies in my corporate account and found that company sponsors the spouse if the stay is more than 6 months and this SPM misguided me in a rush to send me here. Then, I read travel policy which mentioned that compensation is valid only from my company office to client's office and no cab expenses from my home to office.

I started losing trust on my SPM and this company.

One day, I had a spat with South Indian guys at home, because they were demanding rights but did not fulfill their duties — a typical Indian mentality. I used to cook my food separately as usual, but they expected me to do house cleaning. I said common work must be shared.

Slowly we split apart as the student found it difficult to pay the share and other guy had a job change to Germany.

* * *

After searching hard for a suitable room, I found one in nearby location. I was supposed to pay £ 125 per week for such a small accommodation with shared kitchen.

Other options were ruled out and now I started to live with a Polish family. I was worried that they did not know English so how are we going to communicate with each other?

I used sign language first and slowly we became comfortable with each other because they learnt English from me and taught me a little bit of Polish.

They treated me like a family member and not as a tenant. Polish lady used to smoke a lot and take Vodka shots. She also offered me but when I refused she said, "Wow you neither drink nor smoke... Good boy saves money."

Other old lady used to make cake and pizza in the oven. She used to offer me the first bite. She had seen me ordering Domino's pizza, so she knew my likings.

I used to cook with her and his husband used to play guitar. He worked as a Plumber with some construction company.

I was going with the flow but could not forget my love Sagar. Sometimes I used to call him but he did not reply properly. I used to cry day and night. I didn't know why I was so attached to this boy.

In the month of May 2009, tube services were severely affected due to industrial action, which we call 'strike' in Indian terminology.

My SPM emailed me this time and started pressurizing me to go to office anyhow.

I replied back in email that there might be risk involved in my travel and there is no one to look after me in this country if anything goes wrong as I am all alone here.

* * *

In my free time on weekends, I used to visit a friend in East London who consoled me and advised me to search for a better job there. Unfortunately, UK faced severe recession in the year 2009 and all my tries for a better job had failed.

I was just searching Internet for some home based business, when I purchased an online kit for £ 50 by filling my debit card details online. Website provided no option to delete the account and there was an auto-debit option for every month already activated. I searched through contact address and called phone numbers of that rogue company, but I had lost my money and no kit was ever sent to me. I was cheated.

I reported this fraud to my UK bank and they felt sorry for whatever happened. Bank asked me to destroy the card and they issued my new card within 2-3 days and sent it to my UK address free of cost.

Even they credited £ 50 in my account.

I really thanked bank staff for this. I thought what a difference in banking: UK bank has such a big heart that it did not let me suffer for someone else's fraud or my mistake and the Indian banks which even charge for using ATM cards. Charge is okay but at some ATM booths, there is no security person. Facility is not given, only charges are collected.

* * *

One night I got a call from my home in India that my mother got ill while trying hard to search a match for me. Good news was that one party from Jalandar was taking keen interest in me.

I started suffering from physical and mental stress and started shagging 10-15 times per day.

I registered with a GP as I was not feeling well. I was not able to sleep properly. I could not eat properly.

I called and requested my SPM, "Hello madam."

"Yes Rahul?"

"My mother is not well. Please I want to return back to my home or give me the marriage break that you had promised and then I would join back here."

"Oh Rahul, its not possible for next 2 months as I need to prepare someone to take your place and our small project is already suffering resource crunch."

"Please madam..."

"Okay I will write to Thomas Wilson and let us see what can be done."

In acute sexual repression and frustration, I started to search for someone on Internet. I posted an advertisement on a dating website, which I registered from my office email address by mistake.

Next day in the office, client's IT department intercepted responses to my dating advertisement and Thomas Wilson called me in his office.

I left my lunch in-between and went to meet him hurriedly.

"So Rahul, did you give any ad from your office PC on a dating website?"

"No sir, I did not use office PC but a cybercafé."

"Why had you given your office email address?"

"I am really sorry. It was by mistake while filling web form. I will change it."

"You know we have zero tolerance policy for such things in this office. If you were employee of this office, HR had fired you for this. If I complain to your SPM in India, it will spoil your career."

I could understand his concern, but the way he was threatening me for a small mistake was not digestible to me.

I answered boldly, "Okay sir, go ahead. Do what you want to do."

Thomas Wilson was shook from inside and said, "Okay go and delete the advertisement first. Rest I will take care. You were deputed here and not our direct employee. So, no action could be taken against you."

After this incident, I realized how conservative thinking this country has. Their people can publicly kiss on tube stations and bus stops without any problem and if I, who's paying equal tax money as their people, try something to satisfy my physical need, then I am not allowed.

I then thought on what grounds, Thomas Wilson expected me to use my personal laptop for official work.

After this incident, they started scanning every message sent and received by my office computer.

One day I said to Thomas, "Why don't you install a camera above my PC?"

I felt like my needs will break me apart. One Indian gay came to meet at my house one day, but we did not do anything. He shared his experiences of coming and settling in London.

He was an MBA and started his PhD to settle there, but I told him that I am not at all interested to live in the UK for too long.

* * *

I met my GP and I explained how I am getting exploited by client and my company.

Doctor prescribed me some anti-depressant medicine to control my physical stress due to hyper-sexuality, but I used to feel sedated the whole day. Medicine used to relax my body but circumstances were still the same.

In my free time, I used to read all HR policies of my company for India as well as UK. I discovered the online copy of my agreement letter which was not available in my account earlier and was surprised to find that the term for sending me onsite was mentioned as 6 months. I had already been there for one year approximately.

Now I knew how my SPM played smart with me to reduce project cost, because company had to provide some extra money for spouse maintenance as per policy.

Agreement letter given to me mentioned that my onsite term would be one year and could be extended to my visa period of 2 years.

Now, I completely lost trust in company.

My SPM kept lingering me regarding my marriage break for long time without any response. I mailed her my problem and the need to get married.

She called me one day and said, “Rahul you are not in India but in UK. Why don’t you go to brothels and avail the services of prostitutes? Don’t spoil your future and our business.”

I was shocked to hear that and replied, “Sorry, I can’t.”

“You misbehave and use very harsh language in your

email communication with us. Next time, if you did not do what I say, I will complain to senior HR manager and then your career will be at stake."

I replied boldly, "Don't threaten me madam, you can go ahead. Before you think of firing me from this job, I would myself resign. You all are fraud people playing games with my life for your profits."

"Shut up," and my SPM disconnected the call. After this, she never interacted with me.

My doctor knew that I have no friends.

One day I met her on appointment and said, "Doctor my current priority is to get married, but finding a suitable match is getting on my nerves."

Doctor said, "Look Rahul, you are not mentally stable. I would help you as far as possible, but must suggest you that please remain engaged for at least 6 months. A rash choice for life partner could prove wrong and you may suffer your entire lifetime." But this doctor had no idea that Indian middle class marriage is without any dating because society did not allow any openness.

"Thanks doctor for that advice. I will take care."

"How much time I need to take that medicine for my stress problem?"

"If you feel okay, then you can stop tablets after 3-4 months. But such a treatment can go for as long as 6 months to 2 years."

"Thanks doctor. Can I go now?"

"Sure dear, best of luck."

I took a continuous leave of 3-4 days when my HR manager from London office called me on telephone.

"Hello," I said.

"Hello, I am your onsite HR manager and you have to go back to India on 12th August and join back your Indian office."

"But sir, I am not well."

"We are giving you 4 weeks advance notice as mentioned in your agreement letter."

"Okay sir, let me wind up everything."

My onsite HR manager called me personally to London office and explained to me, "Look Rahul, you do not behave well with client. Getting married is your personal problem. You fill out the staff transfer out forms and we complete your tax payment formalities so that you should be ready to go back to India on the date mentioned in your transfer letter."

I said politely, "Sir, I need time to complete my banking formalities and break my phone connection agreement. Please give me some time."

After I came back home, I was hurt by his wrong allegations. SPM did not meet her commitment and this company played foul with me.

Nobody was asking about my health and everyone was just worried about suppressing the truth and making more money for company.

I mailed to HR manager and wrote that I would only go back when I get my last salary credited to my UK bank account. I can not leave things to chance. I will be helpless if something went wrong after I came back to India.

My HR manager replied that I had to go back on that date else that would be treated as my last working day with the company.

I did not go back on the date given as I feared more exploitation. Company was angry with me and I ran into dispute with them.

Behind the scenes, I started saving all the email communication with client and company. I had gone through full immigration policy from UK Border Agency website, and started looking for process of filing a fraud case in court against the company and how they victimized me on the grounds of marriage.

I also wrote my story and sent it via FAX to India's High Commission in UK.

I was all alone there and was worried to get my final salary credited in bank.

Despite all the dispute and apprehensions, company credited my due payments in my UK bank account.

It was the first week of September and HR manager insisted me to buy my air ticket which they would reimburse after I join my office in India.

I replied via email that company had sent me to this place and now it's their responsibility to bring me back. If UK police caught me staying illegally and deported me back, then the company would be responsible.

Company sent me return air tickets. They had used me for money and they also knew very well that I would not join back my Indian office.

* * *

After I came back to India, it was raining heavily and I got sick due to change in weather or climate.

One day, I visited my new office in Gurgaon and my HR manager received me with smiling face and said, "Come on Rahul. I was waiting for you."

"Thanks madam, but I need some time to settle back in this place as you know my hometown is in Punjab, Chandigarh."

"No, you have to join today only as we can not wait more. Should I get your PC ready?"

I thought that this company has no concern for my growth and well being, but earning money is their only concern.

I said, "Don't you think you guys are becoming slaves and doing anything for Dollars and Pounds?"

"Mind your language. You also misbehaved with our client and we have forgiven you for that as your health is not well."

"But who has given you the right to play with my life like this? You forged my onsite agreement for your benefit. Can I ask you why?"

"We did nothing wrong, okay. And don't act over-smart. We did this because we were not confident in your idealistic attitude. This is business and we have to deal with things practically. We were not clear how much time you would stay there and work in a professional way."

"If I had to work professionally, then I would not have done extra work for client. Not only you victimized me on grounds of marriage, but also economically exploited me. Salary that you have mentioned in my visa letter was £ 27,000 per annum and I was actually getting £ 25,350."

"Please no arguments, you are very particular about everything. Tell me what do you want?"

"See madam, my mother is ill and my marriage is a priority for me now. I am not going to prostitutes as my SPM suggested. And if you still think marriage is not important, then why did you marry?" I said pointing to her bangles and *mangal-sutra* (a necklace that married women wear in India) in her neck.

"I have no answers for such stupid questions."

"Okay can you allow me a career break so that I can join after my marriage?"

"No we have no such policy. You will not be entitled any break for marriage as it's your personal thing and if you wish to come back, you will re-join company with fresh round of interview."

"Then I am sorry madam, I am not interested."

"Ok bye." And I came back to Chandigarh the same day.

❑

Eleven

Now I started to have a repulsive feeling for money. I thought what my life has become in pursuit of money. I needed love.

After a few days, I talked to my mother lying on bed, "Are you okay now?"

"Yes I am feeling better," my mother replied with heavy voice.

"I have left my job and not going back to that crooked company."

"Okay, do as you wish."

"Fine, but what about that new girl from Jalandhar? Did you meet them?"

"Yes, but first the girl's parents and her cousin brother with his wife came to see our house. Her mother was ready to do ring ceremony or engagement so that your marriage with their girl was confirmed."

"Very strange as at that time I was in London."

My mother smiled and said, "I also said the same thing

that until my son returns back, who would you do ring ceremony with?"

"Are there any other girls to consider?" I asked.

"Some of them got engaged or married and did not wait for your return. But we have one from local area if you want to meet her first."

"Okay let's meet them this Sunday."

* * *

We met the girl along with her parents and a relative in a park in Panchkula. I don't know why Indian arranged marriages are so formal. Why can't boy and girl meet freely and talk openly so as to know each other well? It seems like relatives and parents are getting married to each other and not boy with girl.

I started talking to girl, "What type of boy you are looking for?"

"One who listens to me and keep me happy always."

I thought this girl seems to be demanding.

Then I asked, "What are you doing these days?"

"I am going to complete my MBA course and searching for some job in a bank. I am preparing for various exams." the girl replied.

"Oh that's really good that you want to be an independent woman."

"What are you looking for?"

"I just wanted a good housewife who could look after my parents and do some job also if she wishes. Do you know cooking?"

"Yes, but I have some conditions..."

"What conditions?"

"I am very religious like my parents and I am strictly vegetarian. I offer prayers to God daily and I do not want anyone to disturb me till I finish."

My mother got to listen this and said, "If your husband needs breakfast in the morning and also expect you to pack lunch for office, then what will you do?"

Girl replied with smiling face, "He also knows cooking."

At this juncture, we came back and thought what type of girls we have these days. It is because of the skewed sex ratio that girls are putting demands on boys. I am UK returned but all my efforts were turning futile.

I met 2-3 girls more but all of them were putting some or the other silly conditions. Marriage was more like a business deal for me now.

* * *

Next day, my mother got a call from Jalandhar.

"Hello."

"Yes."

"I am Dhriti's father from Jalandhar. We had visited your house with matrimonial proposal. Has your son returned back from London?"

"Yes, he's back and in our home these days."

"We would like to meet you."

"Most welcome. Let's meet in a restaurant in Panchkula."

"When?"

"You tell?"

"Let's meet tomorrow only."

"Okay, we shall wait for you."

"Thanks."

My mother clarified to me, "This is the girl from Jalandhar you used to chat with while in London."

"I know mom, but have you ever visited their house after they came here first?"

"Yes son, we have visited their house, but what are your preferences?"

"Nothing special mom; I am not looking for a working wife due to ego clashes, but a good housewife who can handle the household work well. She should be educated enough to work in case need arises and should be of good and adjusting nature, that's all."

"Son, there were maids and servants in their house. Dhriti's mother was handling the kitchen work and cooking."

"Are they very rich?"

"No son, girl's father is a retired government servant but from some good post. But we should concentrate on girl; her behavior was bit odd as we observed."

"Why so mom?"

"She did not get up even once to offer us a glass of water or a cup of tea. Her mother was doing it all."

"May be she was feeling shy at that moment. Bio-data of Dhriti, which her father had sent to me on email, states that she has done M.Sc. (Mathematics) with B.Ed. and now she's about to complete M.Sc. (IT) also. So she is educated enough to a good level. Moreover, she had told me that she worked in a nearby school also. She also knows cooking as she told me in web chat. Her nature is also accommodating. So, I think she's a good match."

"Okay son, let's meet them and decide."

* * *

That day I met Sagar on my way.

I called him, "Hi Sagar, I missed you a lot when I was in London."

Sagar replied, "Okay, but we are just friends now, nothing more."

"You know I loved you more than myself to the extent I can't live without you."

"It's your problem. I can't help it."

"Please dear don't be that insensitive. I would be getting married soon."

"Congratulations! So you should be happy now as you can fulfill your needs now."

"Why would I be happy sweetheart? I am not getting

married to you. Are you sure that you did not love me at all?"

"Stop calling me sweetheart. What is this love drama? A boy can love a girl, but not another boy as my mother told me. I had feelings for you, but now I don't feel like that."

I cried a lot that day. Coincidentally, I was in market and happened to meet Sagar's mother on my way back home.

She was very upset to see me, but I started, "Hello, Auntie Ji. Sagar is not talking to me properly."

"So, what should I do?" she said in very angry tone with her head down and some guilty feeling too.

"Please...you can make him understand my love." I requested.

"Oh God, I have a son and you are crazy about him. What would you have done if he was a girl?" she said mockingly with annoying gestures.

"Excuse me; you think it's a joke. I am suffering from depression after his refusal and taking medicines. He also loved me in the beginning and now left me without any reason. How can he change like that?"

"I am sorry on his behalf. I tried once, but he does not want to have any connections with you." she started shouting.

I left the place as the matter was getting out of control.

Sagar's friends had now started me calling *'gay'* whenever I used to come out of my home.

Around that time only, India legalized homosexuality by amending section 377 and now I faced everyone boldly whoever came in my way to mock at me.

After two days, I was going for jogging or evening walk as part of my daily routine.

Sagar was seen talking to some of my good friends and they started drifting away from me when I came closer. With some of his friends, he started mocking at me with annoying remarks.

"See guys, a *sixer* is coming..." one of the boys in their group shouted.

I kept silent and tried to meet Sagar's father in their house as before.

He came out of the house briefly but did not even open the gate for me and said, "Get lost. I don't have time for you."

After that, I met Sagar alone on road in front of our house and asked him, "If you do not love me its fine, but you have no right to make fun of me publicly like this. Whatever happened between us may be it was love or something else; it was because of our mutual consent. I did not force you for anything. Moreover, you came in my life second time by yourself and before you leave me like this, please give me your replacement as I don't want to die in depression."

"Ha ha, depression..." and he started making gestures to tease me. He was more concerned to look for messages in his cell phone than talking to me.

I was annoyed and took his phone in my hand and said, "Listen Sagar, it's not a joke. I have noticed you many times that whenever I go on road or sit quietly in a park, your friends mock at me and tease me."

"Then why don't you talk to them? I have not asked them to do this with you," Sagar replied.

"Okay, tell me why were you dancing and making comments on me just now?"

"No, where and when?"

"Don't be so innocent. I saw you doing this in front of my house just 10 minutes ago."

While this spat was going on, Sagar slowly called his 2-3 friends and started to act in indecent manner.

"Just give back my mobile phone."

I kept his mobile phone in my trouser's pocket and said, "First you answer my question that why were you mocking at me? Did I say or do anything that caused you to act that way? I loved you and you have already hurt me a lot."

"What should I do? I don't love you."

"Okay, but the question is that why were you making fun of me?"

"I am asking you for the last time; are you giving back my mobile phone or not?" Sagar shouted in anger.

"I will give back your mobile phone only when you answer my question or we go to your parents and I ask you in front of them."

"Don't dare to come to my house again. My father will break your legs, you bloody bitch." saying this Sagar caught my hands from back.

He asked one of his friends to snatch the mobile phone from my pocket. While taking out, phone fell down on ground and was broken.

I got out of the hold of these boys and slapped Sagar. He also backfired and slapped at me.

"You bloody broke my cell phone. Now you will see what happens." Sagar shouted and went back to his house in threatening tone and aggressive mood.

"Yes, you can go. I am waiting..." I replied as I left that place.

Sagar along with his younger brother, parents and a relative started pulling our main gate at night. Time was around 10 pm and they were asking me to come out if I were a man.

I had already told my parents what had happened before they came.

My parents did not open the gate first as they were very agitated. I went to gate and offered them to talk.

Moment I opened the main gate, Sagar's father and mother started slapping me. But I did not back slap anyone.

Sagar's father asked, "Dude, what is your problem?"

"I love Sagar."

Sagar's mother said, "We know the type of love you do, that's why you broke his mobile phone."

I replied, "Auntie Ji, you are mistaken. First, Sagar

started making my fun on road and mobile set got broken as it fell down after my squabble with Sagar's friends."

"Why? Are you a girl that Sagar behaved indecently with you?" Sagar's mother excited me to answer.

"Why are you so hard defining a boy and a girl? Love can be with anyone and indecency can also be with anyone."

They started pushing and beating me again and glass bangles of Sagar's mother broke on my wrist and blood came out. My spectacles were lying crushed on the floor.

Listening to all this drama, my father came out and slapped both Sagar's father and mother and they retaliated.

Sagar interrupted and said to my father, "Uncle don't you dare to touch my parents"

My father replied while pushing them out of our main gate, "How dare your parents come inside my house and beat my family members? You should have talked to me first."

My father also slapped me and said, "I used to advice you to remain away from these cheap guys, but you did not listen to me. See what your love has done. We have been insulted for no fault on our side."

Nobody from my neighbors came out to even see the scene or settle the dispute as everyone is busy and insensitive these days.

Sagar's mother cried, "Why don't you get your son married if he's so hungry for sex? He's after my son from past one year."

My mother replied in shock and pain, "We are trying hard for his marriage already. And if their love affair was going on for one year, why did you not tell us before?"

She replied, "I thought that Rahul is like my son."

"So, what happened now? Can't you forgive him?"

"He has broken my mobile phone and it was worth 10,000 rupees."

I was already in depression and thought in pain... Oh this money has again become more important than my feelings. Everybody is talking about mobile phone that got broken and what about my heart that Sagar had broken so many times by admitting his fake love for me. I said, "If you put so much pressure on me I will commit suicide."

Sagar's parents went back in anger and his mother said, "We are going to lodge a complaint in the police station. This crazy guy is talking nonsense."

Now another scene started in my house after they had left. My father slapped me again and said, "You should better get out of my house and join back your company. You have let us down today. I have not faced so much insult by anyone throughout my life."

I kept silent and applied an antiseptic cream on my wrist.

After sometime, my father and mother went to Sagar's house to pacify the matter, but they had already approached our society's chairman. He was our known, so nothing happened. My parent's good rapport in the society saved us from any further trouble.

* * *

I met Dhriti with her parents who had come with her cousin brother in a restaurant. I asked some questions regarding the household work and surprisingly, her parents were silent from start to finish.

Her cousin brother said, “I can assure you that Dhriti will do every household work.”

I took Dhriti to another table and asked, “Am I okay for you?”

“Yes, do you think I am here for a time pass?” Dhriti replied.

“No, but I need a good housewife. My parent’s health remains down and they have done a lot for me in my life. Now, it’s our turn to support them.” I said.

“Yes, I know cooking as I told you also when we used to chat on Internet.”

“Alright then.”

We had some snacks and then returned back home.

I said to my mother, “Do you think we have a better option?”

“No son. This girl is good enough and should adjust with us easily.”

“I agree that she is educated and polite. But, don’t you think she is not confident enough to work as housewife.”

“All girls we met are like that only. We can wait for a better girl if you are not happy with Dhriti.”

“Mom, I am 29 years old now.”

“Then what... we see in newspapers that there are

many unmarried boys and girls that are aged more than you."

"Mom, we are already struggling for more than 6 years and this society is turning me nuts. I got every quality of a good partner; still I am not getting my match."

"What to do son? You are looking for perfection. See yourself, you may also have flaws."

"I agree mom, but my ideal match would be a boy not a girl."

Mother said in shock, "Are you crazy? Just think of your sister. One day we have to get her married also. What will the people say then? A boy cannot marry a boy, but only a girl."

"Look mom, a boy has got all the qualities of my dream match. He would be independent unlike these dependent girls who expect so much and what we are getting is conditional proposals."

"Okay, how is a boy better? I think you are out of your mind."

"No mom, we have to change with times. A boy would not have that much ego or attitude problem as most of the girls we met had. He would go to a job like me, would know cooking and driving as I do. He will fulfill my needs and we would become a happy couple. A boy can prove to be a better support for you and me. He will save for future and not spend like girls do."

"But; what about your offspring? I want to see your son before I die."

"Mom, please don't talk such rubbish. There are many gay couples living happily and who have adopted babies later."

But my mother, who is just 10th class pass, could not appreciate what gay love means...

"Your thinking and this boy love is beyond my understanding. Did you forget the episode of Sagar and how they created havoc inside our house and insulted us? Your dad is still angry with you. We are already fighting with various diseases and you are creating more tension for us."

"Okay mom, I am ready for marriage with Dhriti. At least you will be happy. I sacrifice for your and sister's sake. I have to follow the norms of this society."

"Okay, but don't blame us afterwards."

"It's fine mom. I have to follow the family system or live separately. But you have done so much for me. I can't leave you."

"I love you son." my mother concluded.

Then I called Dhriti's father and said, "Hello, Dhriti?"

"Yes, I am Dhriti's father."

"I am Rahul."

"Yes Rahul?"

"Sir, I am ready for marriage with your daughter."

"That's great. Is there any demand from you or your family?"

"Excuse me sir. We do not expect any favor, money

or gifts. All that I want is simple marriage and a good housewife."

"Okay then, we should start making arrangements."

"Thank you." I concluded.

"Take care son, Bye." Dhriti's father ended the call with happy tone.

I thought that I have made a wrong decision in haste, but circumstances were like that and there was no alternative.

I said to my father, "Now your tension will be solved. But can you call and ask Dhriti's father for engagement or ring ceremony as I am doubtful that such a fast track marriage is not suitable."

"What the hell are you talking about? Why are you so confused? You tell me if you want to marry or not?" my father said in aggressive tone.

My mother interrupted, "Why are you getting hyper? Just ask Dhriti's father if my Rahul wants that way..."

In the evening, Dhriti's father called on his own.

I picked the phone and said, "Yes uncle."

"Dhriti is planning to fill forms for MCA. Should she proceed?"

"Sir, she is already having two master degrees, so why on earth we want her to do another Masters?"

"Okay, give phone to your father?" and he repeated the same question to my father.

My father said, "Sharma ji, please focus on marriage ceremony. Can I request you something?"

"Yes, sure."

"We want engagement first and let us do the ring ceremony that you wanted to do initially."

"That's fine. Let me talk to others in my home about it. But is the marriage confirmed from your side or not?"

"Yes sir, please take your time and tell us."

"Dhriti is also agreeing to this alliance. Okay ji, bye."

That was marriage season and literally we were unable to find any marriage palace or community center to perform the ceremony.

Dhriti's cousin brothers and family did make fast arrangements and just one day before the marriage date, Dhriti's father called my father.

"Hello, can I talk to Rahul's father?"

"Yes Sharma ji?"

"I have made full arrangement for Dhriti's marriage with Rahul in Jalandhar only. It was tough but we made it."

"Okay, but what about the ring ceremony and engagement?"

"Oh ring ceremony is just a formality that we can perform in marriage function itself. I have spent a lot of money, so please don't back out now."

"Sir, we have also distributed wedding cards. I was making arrangement here."

"How many relatives do you expect to come as I have to tell this to my catering guys?"

“We have given out 50 wedding cards but we expect only 15-20 relatives to attend our marriage function.”

“You know my list of relatives is around 80-100 people. Its cost effective if you come to Jalandhar in place of me coming to Chandigarh.”

“Okay sir, as you wish.”

“Thank you; you are really a nice person.”

So, my father became an emotional fool by this smart and cunning person.

❑

Twelve

My marriage with Dhriti was solemnized in the month of November, 2009 as per Hindu customs. Everything was just fine and appeared normal except one thing; Dhriti did not seem to be happy throughout the marriage function. She had an artificial smile as seen in the wedding movie also.

Dhriti's relatives had thronged the marriage palace and made me so busy in customs that I could not observe this thing too closely.

Dhriti's father kept asking my father again and again with a paper in his hand, "Sharma ji, I have got a list of items like LCD TV, Washing Machine, Refrigerator, Bed and Sofa. So, please let me know what I should purchase for Dhriti's house."

My father joined his hands together and said, "Sharma ji, you have already seen my house. With God's grace we already have everything we need. If there is something we need, my son will buy that himself. We are strictly against dowry. So, please don't offer us anything. We just want a good daughter-in-law who respects and cares for us."

"Oh that's not dowry, but gift. How can I send my daughter empty handed?"

"Please sir; we don't want anything from you. You have already done so much for marriage arrangement."

"No, it's only with the support of my relatives that such function was possible."

"Still, please..."

"Okay, no problem. As you wish." my father-in-law concluded.

After the marriage function ended, we brought Dhriti to our home.

* * *

After a few hours of rest, I asked Dhriti, "How did you find my parents and this home, I mean, what's your first impression?"

"They are nice and your house is also very clean and organized."

"Thanks Dhriti, but it is now your house as well."

"I know."

"And now you should be taking care of this house and my family as your own. Can I ask you something if you don't mind?"

"Yes ask."

"Mostly the girls weep a lot in *beedai* (girl's separation from her family) and I did not find even a single tear in your eyes when you were seated in the car we came in. Your relatives and parents were crying though."

"No nothing like that. My heart was heavy. I do not believe in show off."

"Okay, no issues."

On my first night, I tried to get romantic with her but she was not comfortable as though she did not like my looks or we were total strangers, meeting for the first time.

I said with excitement, "This is the night which most boys in India dream of…"

"Rahul, is this the only relation between a husband and wife?"

"Oh what do you mean?" I asked in surprise.

"Let's live as brother and sister or you can say friends."

I was shocked to my bones and said, "Oh shit, do you think marriage is a joke? I have no option now but to file a divorce case and I would get it easily as it's a fraud that you have done with me."

"No I need some more time to understand you."

"What the fuck Dhriti? What more understanding do you want? We used to chat almost daily when I was in London and I also told you that I had a boy friend in my life that I loved more than myself. Now, I will make one new boy friend and then get my satisfaction from him. I don't need you."

My wife was shocked to hear all this and tried to console me.

I put her hand away and said, "Please don't touch me."

"Oh I was joking. Please don't take my words to heart. Do what you want."

Love making happened with no involvement from her side.

Next day, I noted that she was not taking any interest in the household work and my sister and mother kept working in kitchen.

My wife asked while sitting on her bed, "Can you get me a glass of water?"

I said, "Okay."

Then, I thought something is seriously wrong.

After drinking water, she said, "I am missing my home. Let's go to Jalandhar."

I said, "It's already 2 pm and even if we get a bus from Chandigarh bus stand in time, it will reach there late at night. We will go tomorrow in morning time so that we can reach in day time only because the travel time from our house to your place is around 5 hours."

"Okay," she said with a sad expression.

* * *

I visited my in-laws house for the first time. They showed me their old house and shops in Jalandhar's *Atari*

Bazaar (market place) and told me how they lived together in a joint family.

Dhriti said, "My father has progressed very well and see now we are in a new house. He has spent his entire retirement money on this house."

"What is your younger brother doing?" I asked.

"Oh he fell in bad company once and could not complete his studies. He just sits in my cousin brother's shop and helps them in their business."

"It means he is earning, good."

"But my household expenses are met by my father's pension and the pension amount is good enough."

"Okay, that's great."

Dhriti's mother remained in kitchen and prepared several dishes for me. Cleaning and washing jobs were being carried out by maids. I saw their house to be very untidy unlike ours, which is better maintained and organized.

Most of the time, Dhriti kept watching TV sitting on her sofa in drawing room.

My in-laws treated me very well and my mother-in-law insisted that I should stay for some more time even after my four days stay. I said, "I have to try for a new job. Please let us go now, we shall come again later."

After we were back to my house, our relatives and my wife's local relatives started inviting us one by one for lunch and dinner — a custom for newly wedded couples.

After a few days, some aunties from our neighborhood came to see my wife.

My wife did not move from the sofa she was sitting on and kept on looking at her nail paint and rotating the handkerchief she had in her hands.

I quickly went to kitchen and prepared tea for guests.

After aunties had left, I said to Dhriti in soft voice, "You should have asked these women a glass of water or tea at least. What impression will they get from you? They were our guests."

"I don't care for outside people." my wife replied.

Then I talked to my mother in her room, "Mom, I don't know but the way Dhriti behaves in her house is not seen here. She behaves indifferent as if this house is a hotel."

"Don't worry son. Slowly she will adjust to our house. You have to care for her so that she feels attached to us."

For next few days also, my wife kept denying physical relation.

One day in the month of December, I talked to my mother about it and she said, "Should I bring this matter to your in-laws notice?"

"I suggest let me talk to Dhriti first as things may get against us."

I tried to talk to my wife openly but she diverted the topic and said, "Let's go to Jalandhar. I need to bring back some gifts that my relatives had given to me on our wedding."

I took the bus in afternoon and reached my in-laws house at night.

My in-laws were very happy to see their daughter back. They kept me busy in one or other thing.

I said, "Dhriti I have to go back to my home now. You can come back on your own after few days."

Dhriti said, "No, I will get ready."

While she got to washroom, she just threw her gold rings on bed, taking off from her three fingers one by one.

I asked my mother-in-law, "Is Dhriti so careless? These are three gold rings and she is throwing them like that..."

My mother-in-law replied with a smiling face, "Now, you have to take care of her and her things."

I thought that I have seriously got a wrong partner, who cannot even take care of herself. How would she take care of me and my parents if she is that careless?

"What she likes to do?"

"She is fond of watching Shahrukh Khan Movies and his songs on TV."

"Okay what about the household work?" I asked in surprise.

"We have maids. You also hire some servants," my mother-in-law replied in assertive way.

I kept silent and then came back to my home and told everything to my mother. I had to pack her luggage myself and Dhriti did nothing in her house.

My mother was speechless and kept staring at Dhriti with surprise.

I asked Dhriti one day, "Don't you see my mother and sister working throughout the day. Don't you think that you should go and help them in kitchen?"

She entered into kitchen in angry mood only when my mother asked her for preparing rice. She was upset and said, "Your pressure cooker is different from ours. Its faulty and I can't cook in this."

She came back to sit on bed in our room and I asked, "What happened?"

"I have no interest in cooking."

I was shocked and said, "But you said in our online chat that you can cook well and that you are going to join cooking class before marriage."

"Yes, but I was not well at that time."

"Okay Dhriti, let my sister cook food and my mother is already washing my clothes. Can you just focus on cleaning work?"

"Oh your house is so big? I can't handle it."

That day only I purchased a vacuum cleaner and started telling Dhriti how to operate that, but she was not interested to learn anything.

I fell into deep depression for the fraud these people have done with me. I got suspicious of her M.Sc. (Mathematics) degree. Mathematics is a logical subject, then how can such a dumb pass that degree?

I asked Dhriti, "I think you are not good at household work. This time when you go back to your parent's home just bring your educational certificates and experience letter where you used to work."

"Okay."

After a few days, Dhriti said, "I am missing my home. I want to meet my parents."

I said, "Look Dhriti, we have already been there two times. After marriage, this is your house and not your parents' house. You live here as if we have kept you in a hotel and opened a restaurant for you. If you are so attached to Jalandhar, you should have married a local guy."

Dhriti replied in angry tone, "Okay, but I can't leave my parents for you. I am attached to my father and he also loves me a lot."

I packed her luggage and made her sit in the bus for Jalandhar because I did not want any dispute.

I started to feel a lot of mental stress as physical needs also remain unfulfilled.

I returned back to my home and said to my mother, "I don't know what Dhriti is doing. If she is so comfortable in her house, then why she married me? Why don't you say anything to her?"

My mother replied, "Son, now you are mature enough to take care of things at your level. Don't say anything to us now."

My father said, "I am going to retire in the month of April, 2010 and would be unable to run household as before because I have no money. Rahul, do some job. Why are you sitting idle at home?"

I thought everyone is thinking about themselves and nobody has any idea about what I am going through. I continued to take the antidepressant medicine prescribed by that London doctor to keep myself in control.

I left industry and joined back education field. I was easily appointed in my college as they knew me well.

I received a few backdated letters to join back my company in Gurgaon and the last letter said that I had left job on my will.

After few days, I received a legal notice that I have not resigned properly and need to pay back some sum of money (Rupees 12,000 to be specific) as final settlement.

I replied with my full story to company's private advocate in an email and said, "Company can deduct my PF account which has Rupees 35,000 deposited in it. And I don't want any money from anyone as it spoiled my life. You can keep the balance amount also. I am in depression."

Advocate felt sorry after knowing the whole story and did not call me again.

* * *

After a couple of days, my wife came back with her brother. We told Dhriti's behavior to her brother and he had no answer either.

One night somebody called on my wife's phone and said, "Dheeru, talk to me, please don't disconnect the call."

I asked my wife, "Who is that fellow?"

My wife replied, "Must be a wrong number. I don't know."

"Don't tell a lie. If it was wrong number, how the guy knew your name? Please call back this number and I will ask who he is. Did you have any affair with anyone before marriage?"

"No nothing like that."

"See I told you about my affair very openly before marriage. You can also tell me, I promise I will not tell anyone." I assured her.

"One boy used to chase me while I was in college, but he was not of our caste."

"But was he Hindu?"

"Yes."

"Oh God, you idiot! Why did you not marry him if he loved you so much?"

"No he was just after sex only."

"Okay, forget it. I don't care. But you should not go to Jalandhar so quickly again and again."

"Fine I want to sleep now."

For few days, my mother taught Dhriti household work and tried to adjust her. My sister also helped her, but she showed no interest or progress.

She turned my room into total mess and did not even wash her clothes for a month. When I asked the reason, she replied, "I would get my clothes dry cleaned when I go back to my home this time."

One day I asked her to do some dusting of the bed we sleep on and the TV she watched and she replied, "You should hire a maid. I am not your servant."

I said in utter surprise, "Dhriti then am I servant or my family members are servants? It's our work and we are doing it. This time when you come back, bring you educational and experience certificates without fail."

"You cannot force me to do a job." my wife replied.

"Oh really, you can't do a job. You can not perform your housewife duties. Physically you have no emotions for me. Then, what are you doing in my life? What am I getting in this relationship?"

My wife started crying and said, "I want to go to my father's home."

"Stop acting like a kid Dhriti. You are not going anywhere till the time my parents and I am happy with you."

"I have not done marriage to satisfy anybody. Your expectations are too high."

"Dhriti, our expectations are not high. You have not learnt anything throughout your life and not even interested to learn anything now."

"You won't go anywhere till you learn and adjust to the system of our house."

After this; my disgruntled wife started keeping lights on and flushed out the whole water from water tank one day.

I was totally shattered with her misbehavior and said, "Okay, you can go to Jalandhar tomorrow."

She packed her luggage that day only. I was sedated with anti-depressant drugs as usual. I did not eat anything the whole day.

I was so much stressed with all this drama that to reduce my stress, I did unsafe sex with her without realizing that her periods were on. It was the first week of February 2010, when she left our house.

* * *

After a few days, Dhriti called me on phone, "Hello Rahul, how are you?"

"I am fine and you must be happy in your home, right?"

"Yes, but I need to tell you something very important."

"What's that?"

"I am pregnant."

"What? Are you serious?" I asked in surprise.

"Yes, my periods had stopped and then I along with my cousin sister visited a doctor. My pregnancy is confirmed."

"Oh God, please take some pills and we would not go to the abortion stage."

"Why? You always wanted a child."

"Yes Dhriti, but it is not the right time. We already married in hurry and you have not still adjusted in our house. Even I and my family are not satisfied with how our relationship is going."

"Do you want a son?"

"No, whatever it is; son or daughter, we can have a child later when our relationship becomes stable. Having a kid is big responsibility and we are not prepared for it. Please try to understand me."

"I know you don't love me and I am also not comfortable with you. So, this child is only my support. It's a sin to kill someone before birth."

"Dhriti, please don't be idealistic. We are already facing so many practical problems in our life. I don't want my baby to face the problems that I had to face because of this corrupt system. This country can not provide employment and if we can't give our child a better future, what's the use of bringing him or her in this world for suffering?"

"Rahul, every child has his destiny and can't you provide him three times meals and some clothing?"

"Dear I can provide but I am not mentally prepared. I don't want him to suffer like I did."

"I know your love for boys. Why did you not marry a boy? You spoiled my whole life."

"Stop that Dhriti. My life is also spoiled. I had married a boy if law had provisions, this society permitted and my parents could accept my love."

"I don't know. That's your problem. I will give birth to this child."

I disconnected the phone and started remaining tense. I had finished my anti-depressant medicine. I tried many Homeopathic and Ayurvedic medicines, but all in vain.

Dhriti returned after a month, so nothing could be done now. I had to get her tests done from a doctor of my in-laws choice, so that nobody could blame me if something went wrong.

My mother and sister tried their level best to teach Dhriti all household work.

One day I said to my wife, "See Dhriti, this is not a coaching center. Your mother is such a good cook. Why did you not learn anything from her?"

Dhriti was quick to reply back, "She has done her Home Science course and your sister has so many years of experience. Don't compare me to her."

"Okay, how much time you need? I have to go to office in the morning and catch the bus at 8 am. But you never make it in time. I asked for your certificates so that we can find you a job, but you do not listen to us."

"Shame on you; I am pregnant."

"That's why I asked you not to bear baby. You always find excuses to hide your inabilities or shirk work for one or other reasons. I am in depression as you see but I am not sitting at home. I have so much of back pain; still I am doing my job."

"Then you should hire a cook if you don't like my cooking or timing."

"Wow, your mother advised me to hire maids and now cook. Do you think that you are married to a millionaire?"

"Maid is not that costly that you can't afford."

"Yes, but we are independent and do our work on our own. Mine is a small family of four family members only and not a joint family. You are never expected to handle all the tasks yourself, but you are not even good at handling simple things. Why are you so mentally weak and physically feeble?"

"Don't pressurize me; else I would file a harassment case and a dowry case against you."

"Oh really? When did we ask anything from you or your parents?"

"I am not interested to talk about anything. I do not want to fight."

"Even I am not interested in you."

After some hours, while washing clothes in washing machine along with my mother, Dhriti started putting her hands inside the running machine. She started behaving careless either to hurt her or warn us.

That day I sent a text (sms) message to girl's brother to take her from our home as she was not listening to us.

It was the month of July, 2010 and the next day, Dhriti's father along with three relatives came to my house when I was not present in house and started threatening my parents with dire consequences. Then, they took my wife in their car at night along with her luggage.

My sober looking wife acted so smart that she was taking all the jewelry without telling anyone. It would act as a key to call me later to their house.

My mother acted swiftly and took back our part of jewelry.

There was no call from either side for a long time.

* * *

My parents and sister visited my wife in hospital where my mother-in-law said, "We wanted Rahul to be here. We will send Dhriti only when he comes to take her, else not."

My wife had given birth to a baby boy in October, 2010, but I was not happy with anything and anyone. I had just become a puppet of these people and this bloody system.

I started to take antidepressant medicine from a good Government hospital.

Whenever my father-in-law called, I told him that I was not well.

In the month of November, 2011, my wife filed a complaint against me and my family members. We got a call from the office of Additional Deputy Commissioner of Police (ADCP), Jalandhar to attend the hearing and present our viewpoint.

We were present on the scheduled date time and made an entry in their attendance register.

Reader of ADCP directed us to wait till girl's party came.

In the office of ADCP, the reader asked me, "So what is the problem?"

"Sir, we are here on you verbal calls. Please can you tell me what the complaint is all about and I will explain you all the points one by one."

ADCP laughed and said in aggressive tone, "We are asking you something and how dare you ask us back?"

"Sorry sir, but I really don't know what the complaint is..."

"Haven't my reader shown you the copy of complaint?"

"No sir."

"Okay reader, tell him."

Reader spoke, "You have not come to meet your wife for past one year and even see your baby. Why?"

I replied, "I was in depression and have a back pain even now. I came as it was urgent else I don't even travel."

"That's an excuse. Tell us the truth. Why are you in depression?" ADCP inquired.

"Sir, my wife does not seem to be happy from day one of the marriage. She is not comfortable having physical relation with me. She does not respect my parents and does not take any interest in doing or learning any household work. Even she is not interested to do any job."

"What you do gentleman?" ADCP asked.

"I am working as an Assistant Professor in a college."

"What's your salary?"

"I earn approx. Rupees 20,000 per month after tax deductions."

"Ok, but you are supposed to fulfill your matrimonial responsibilities. Now you have a baby and it's legitimate, right?"

"Yes sir, I am ready. But, Dhriti should also fulfill her responsibilities. I only gave her time to learn things like cooking as she also needed time to change."

ADCP then asked my wife, "Dhriti, what's the issue?"

Dhriti replied, "Sir I worked very well in their house, but the nature of my in-laws is too bad."

My sister asked, "Dhriti can you tell even a single instance when we scolded or abused you or even spoke in loud voice?"

Dhriti said in aggressive tone, "Shut up."

ADCP took serious note of this behavior and asked my wife, "Wait a minute, what is your qualification girl?"

My wife replied, "M. Sc., B. Ed."

ADCP said in angry tone, "You are sitting in the office of commissioner and don't even know how to behave with your in-laws. And yes, I also noted that girl's father did not stop Dhriti. I think she is also out of her father's control."

After this ADCP directed us to sit outside and kept talking to my wife's relatives for about half an hour in a closed room.

I had guessed that they were working on instructions of somebody from my wife's extended family or relatives.

Dhriti's cousin brother came out and took me to a corner. He said, "Rahul let's settle the matter and negotiate."

"What should I agree to sir? You have not fulfilled even a single commitment you made before marriage. Dhriti can neither cook nor drive even a 2-wheeler. How am I expected to take full responsibility of her and the child?"

"Then, do you want divorce?"

"No I got married after a long struggle of six years. I would neither give her divorce nor take divorce. She has to adjust as per our system."

"Okay let me talk to Dhriti at home and then I will call you back."

"Alright." and we came back to our house.

* * *

My father was scared too much. My mother started to weep and said, "See now our children have brought us to police stations without any fault of ours. Someone in neighborhood told me that one innocent in-law family died in jail when their daughter-in-law implicated them in a false dowry case."

I said, "Don't worry mom, everything will be alright."

My father said, "What will be alright? They will file F.I.R. and put us in jail."

"Okay I will do something. I will take legal advice from an advocate."

My colleague referred me to a good advocate, whom I told the full story of my marriage and reason for breakage.

I said, “Sir, ADCP and his associates are working on girl’s family directives. They are neither showing nor providing us the copy of complaint. I doubt that they will implicate us in false dowry case.”

Advocate got me a direction notice from Punjab and Haryana High Court that I should be provided a copy of F.I.R. or complaint, if any.

When I appeared before that ADCP on the date written on court order, he had already got the copy of the court notice. One more advocate accompanied me in case an anticipatory bail was required.

ADCP said to me, “You think you are very smart or something?”

I said, “Sorry sir, what did I do?”

“Why you had to go to High court? Did we say anything wrong to you when you came here last time?”

“Sir, your reader was not providing us the copy of complaint.”

“Then you should have given application under RTI Act. But you took action against me and my associates.”

“Sorry sir, I had no such intention. My advocate advised me like this only.”

“Just read the court order which says that I have full right to interrogate you for Dhriti’s complaint and then record your statements.”

“Sir, you also directed to record our statements last time we came, but your reader did not attend to us properly and we had to return back.”

In the mean time, reader called girl's party.

"Settle your dispute if you want or we take next step. I have many other important tasks to do." ADCP went away saying.

That day I met my baby boy on being pressurized by wife's relatives.

My advocate asked Dhriti in all possible ways but neither had she accepted her share of responsibilities nor did she open up to accept the hard truth of my inclination or limitations. She's just interested in my time and money that I can give her.

All involved in the dispute resolution had given up and then we returned back our home late at night in puzzled, confused and frustrated state.

I spent Rupees 50,000 in all this legal drama and corrupt system.

May God save innocent people from the worst system of this country!

May God bless us all!

❑

Epilogue

Nancy said, "Oh dear, that's a mind boggling story! You know all this mess could have been avoided."

"How? Do you think changing the mindsets of typical middle-class people of India and this corrupt system are so simple and easy tasks?"

"No change can come overnight. But at least we can make people aware about things."

"You are right. How do you analyze this story?"

"See if India had legalized gay marriage as we have done, Rahul could have married to a boy partner of his choice and the whole story would have been different. In place of this misery, love and happiness would have prevailed. Now, Dhriti and baby would have to suffer throughout their lives as Rahul is unable to attach himself emotionally to them."

"Don't you think open culture and effects of globalization have eroded our family system here?"

"Dear yours is an overly populated country and resources are difficult to distribute evenly. So, managing all the things well is very difficult. Computers and new technology are helping to manage systems better, but have their drawbacks at the same time. In olden times, people used to meet. Now, we have social networking websites. Times have changed."

"In case of Rahul, root cause of his problem is that abuser."

"No, he is not the root cause but a fanatic who lacked self control. Like Rahul, he might have also undergone similar abuse and stress. What do you suggest for such MNCs and guys joining these companies?"

"I suggest single guys to get married before they join a big company as they would not give them time for marriage later. Moreover, MNCs and call centers that employ single guys and girls as their preference; should permit open and free sex. Nancy but what should our government do to make things better?"

"Legalize prostitution as soon as possible and tax this service like any other service. But problem is to take your religious leaders, fundamentalists and conservative culture savers into confidence."

"Are you crazy? India will never do that. Has any country ever done that?"

"Yes dear. Prostitution is legal (with some restrictions that aren't that bad) in Canada, most of Europe including England, Scotland, Poland, Netherlands, France, Wales, Denmark, etc., most of South America including most of Mexico, Brazil, Israel (Tel Aviv known as the brothel capital of the world), Australia, New Zealand, Singapore and many others. It is either legal or much tolerated in almost all of Asia and even Iran has *temporary wives*, which can be for only a few hours!"

"Okay, but what would be the benefit of such legalization?"

"Take smoking and drinking for example. Governments tried to ban it and still things continued undercover. Many foreign countries legalized the same and started collecting heavy taxes. They spend that money on needy, but you have corrupt leaders. Nevertheless, crime rates would go down. Similarly, if we legalized prostitution, guys will have an outlet to release the extra energy in place of raping 2 year olds like this. You know why guys are turning gay?"

"I don't know about situation in your country. But in our North Indian states, the male to female ratio was 1000:900 ten years ago and now it's fallen down to 1000:700 approximately, mostly due to killing of female fetus. Its simple logic: 700 boys could marry 700 girls, but what about (1000 — 700) = 300 boys we are left with? They have no choice, but will have to either compete for girls or become gays to satisfy themselves."

"Right."

"Okay, how can your solution have worked in Rahul's story?"

"Most people who think they are bisexual are in fact gays. If Rahul had a chance to do sex with a girl before marriage and he knew that he's not going to click with a girl, but only with a boy who can fulfill his foot fetish, whole story would have turned in to a happy living and not a forced slavery of this failed marriage."

"Most marriage and divorce laws in India go against males."

"Yes that needs a change too. Your government must do something. Why to keep running a failed or broken marriage?"

"Do you think love marriages are better then?"

"Yes, if these are done before 25 years, else marriage has high probability to fail either due to high expectations of love before suitable time or be successful due to higher maturity levels later. There is no guarantee even in the best system we may devise. But we should keep learning from experiences and improve things."

"But Rahul's marriage was neither love nor arranged marriage. It was a business marriage done to fulfill needs on both sides and reference source was a newspaper. If Rahul and Dhriti were given enough time for dating and engagement, which is not a norm in Indian culture unfortunately, they might have not entered into relationship that fast and averted the things as they are now. We say marriages are made in heaven..."

Nancy laughed and said, "And such marriages succeed only in heaven as ground reality is different. By the way what is Rahul's next plan?"

"He is looking for a gay partner and waiting to marry with his soul-mate once gay marriage is legalized in India. In the mean time, he has to lead a dual life. Do you know countries that have totally legalized gay system?"

"Of course I know. Netherlands was the first country to accept this fully with gay marriages legalized. Other countries in the list are Canada, UK, Brazil, South Africa, Norway, Sweden, Portugal, and Spain."

"Thanks for that information. How did you know?"

"My fiancé's friends are mostly gays and they are open with me. I wish Rahul best of luck for his gay partner search."

"But Rahul is not a hardcore gay. He's just foot fetish. Anyways, thanks."

Train reached Chandigarh railway station and we got down at platform number one. Nancy shook hands with me and bid me good bye.

SELF HELP

YES, YOU CAN

INDIA BOOK OF RECORDS 2016

Management Guru
LORD KRiSHNA
Tips for achieving
Paritranaya Sadhunaam
Vinashaya Cha Dushkritaam
Dharmasansthapanarthaya Sambhavaami Yuge Yuge
O.P. Jha

No Dream Too Big
BELIEVE IN DETERMINATION
Joginder Singh

DYNAMIC MEMORY
SURE SUCCESS IN INTERVIEWS
Tarun Chakarborty

DYNAMIC MEMORY
GROUP DISCUSSION
Tarun Chakarborty

Time Management
Dr. Rekha Vyas

108 INCOME-TAX MANTRAS FOR TAX SAVING
Subhash Lakhotia

TIPS OF PROPERTY
Buying, Selling, Renting & Tax Planning
R.N. LAKHOTIA. SUBHASH LAKHOTIA

SUBHASH LAKHOTIA
TAX GURU
HOW TO BECOME A MILLIONAIRE
Practical Money Making Ideas for Complete Financial Freedom

ASHU DUTT
Market Guru and Bestselling Author
MASTER THE STOCK MARKET

Jolly Uncle
Stories that Enlighten You
JPS Jolly

DARE TO DREAM DARE TO EXCEL
• Never give up.
• Make your own fate.
• Determination is the key to success.
• The power to succeed lies within you.
Dr. Harikrishna Devsare

HEAL WITHOUT PILL
Incurable⇨Cure within
Dr. Biswaroop Roy Chowdhury

108 INVESTMENT MANTRAS
Time Tested Tips For Beneficial Investment

Badminton Queen of India
Saina Nehwal